Praise for *You Don't Need Superpowers to Be a Kid's Hero*

What an innovative approach to highlighting and demystifying the work we do as school leaders at all levels! If you've every dreamed of flying, having super strength, or being invisible, and you engage in the worthy work of building up young minds, this is the book for your. Bill Ziegler and Dave Ramage provide great examples and models for the best "super-hero" traits we have and use to make bold differences. Excelsior!

Derek McCoy
Award-Winning Principal and Author

Once again, Bill Ziegler and Dave Ramage have nourished the profession with a fearless and compelling compilation of anecdotes, strategies, rubrics, and inspiration that will benefit any school leader. Every child needs a hero and every child can be a hero. This work highlights real-life heroes in our schools and how to build heroes in students and teachers. Read these stories and engage these heroes on your social networks to build your encouragement network. I am most excited to take away and use their tools for increasing student voice and choice to make my school even better!

Carrie Jackson
Principal
Northwest High School, Justin, TX
Texas Association of Secondary School Principals State Coordinator

In this deeply inspiring book, Ziegler and Ramage show educators how they can have a positive impact on all of the students in their schools. Superheroes are no longer just for movies; they are real people and have real stories illustrated in this book.

Peter DeWitt, EdD
Author/Consultant

Bill Ziegler and Dave Ramage have written a must-read book for today's school leaders! Their commitment and dedication to creating positive cultures will inspire school leaders to make real life changes in their practice that impact staff, students, and the entire school community. They equip and empower you to build heroes in your schools to change our world for the better.

Matt Moyer
Principal of Rupert Elementary School
Principals of Learning

Bill Ziegler and Dave Ramage remind us of what's most important—our students. And they remind us of our ultimate purpose—inspiring and empowering those students to thrive. As Gandhi challenged us to "be the change we wish to see," Ziegler and Ramage challenge us with the reality that "leadership carries a moral purpose." We are changing lives! We are shaping the future! *You Don't Need Superpowers to Be a Kid's Hero* is immensely practical. It features the stories of school leaders who are doing the great work now! It is a handbook for school leaders everywhere who are committed to building cultures in their schools that allow their students to soar.

Danny Steele
Award-Winning Principal, Author, and Professor at University of Montevallo

Ziegler and Ramage continue to up the leadership ante with their latest book, *You Don't Need Superpowers to Be a Kid's Hero*. Another book for the leader in all of us, it hits on key needle-moving points about the need for relationship, innovation, and voice and choice for our learners. The voice and choice chapter forces educators to include our kids in decisions. This book talks empowerment! In these chapters you will find practical pieces to implement from the ones that know the current vibe of education—practitioners! The book also has great tools for reflection that helps us to ask the tough questions of *why* and *how*.

Darren Ellwein, Award-Winning Middle School Principal and Author of *The Revolution: It's Time to Empower Change in Our Schools*

You Don't Need Superpowers to Be a Kid's Hero is empowering and practical. Ramage and Ziegler write from a place of deep credibility and their latest take on servant leadership is sure to inspire. To top it off, the vast cadre of school leaders they feature will not only help you hone in on your *why*, but they will help you with your *how*—making this one of the most actionable school leadership titles I've seen.

Brad Gustafson, Award-Winning Principal and Author

Real heroes shatter the status quo and build cultures where students and staff are loved and supported each day. In this inspiring book, Bill Ziegler and Dave Ramage share stories of successful hero-builders who inspire us to change the world, one kid at a time. If you want to live up to your hero status, read this book and implement the powerful practice in your school immediately. Your students and staff will thank you!

Salome Thomas-EL, Principal and Author

The world of education is hard. It is sometimes difficult to find the positives in what we do. Although I do not believe that any educator gets into education to be a superhero, I think educators need to see how our work is extraordinary—not because we set out to be extraordinary but because we find our work meaningful, personal, and rewarding. This book highlights practical ideas from people working in the field of education. It calls attention to some of the little things that have made incredible impacts on their students, schools, and communities. Bill Ziegler and Dave Ramage have done an outstanding job helping to remind educators of why they became educators, inspired people to some new perspectives, offered encouragement, and given us a call to action that our superpowers are making a difference in the lives of our students every day.

Mariah Rackley, Award-Winning Middle School Principal

In the busy world of the principalship, leaders must realize the power within themselves to design and implement strategies that capitalize on the strengths of the school community. In their book, *You Don't Need Superpowers to Be a Kid's Hero: Leading a Hero-Building School Culture*, Ziegler and Ramage's concept of Hero Sightings, Hero Training, and Hero Simulations is a genius way to put practical strategies in the hands of school leaders through reflective activities at the end of each chapter. A true resource for principals who believe in their powers to transform their school community.

Mary Pat Cumming
Principal, The FAIR School
Minneapolis Public Schools

You Don't Need Superpowers to Be a Kid's Hero

You Don't Need Superpowers to Be a Kid's Hero

Leading a Hero-Building School Culture

Bill Ziegler

Dave Ramage

Foreword by Jessica Cabeen

FOR INFORMATION:

Corwin
A SAGE Company
2455 Teller Road
Thousand Oaks, California 91320
(800) 233-9936
www.corwin.com

SAGE Publications Ltd.
1 Oliver's Yard
55 City Road
London, EC1Y 1SP
United Kingdom

SAGE Publications India Pvt. Ltd.
B 1/I 1 Mohan Cooperative Industrial Area
Mathura Road, New Delhi 110 044
India

SAGE Publications Asia-Pacific Pte. Ltd.
18 Cross Street #10-10/11/12
China Square Central
Singapore 048423

Printed in Great Britain by Ashford Colour Press Ltd.

Library of Congress Cataloging-in-Publication Data

Names: Ziegler, Bill, author. | Ramage, Dave, author.

Title: You don't need superpowers to be a kid's hero: leading a hero-building school culture / Bill Ziegler, Dave Ramage.

Description: First edition. | Thousand Oaks, California : Corwin, a SAGE company, [2020] | Includes bibliographical references.

Identifiers: LCCN 2019047063 | ISBN 9781544355085 (paperback) | ISBN 9781544355108 (epub) | ISBN 9781544355115 (epub) | ISBN 9781544355122 (ebook)

Subjects: LCSH: Educational leadership—United States. | School management and organization—United States.

Classification: LCC LB2805 .Z42 2020 | DDC 371.2—dc23

LC record available at https://lccn.loc.gov/2019047063

This book is printed on acid-free paper.

Publisher: Arnis Burvikovs
Acquisitions Editor: Ariel Curry
Development Editor: Desiree Bartlett
Associate Editor: Eliza Erickson
Production Editor: Gagan Mahindra
Copy Editor: Michelle Ponce
Typesetter: Hurix Digital
Proofreader: Sally Jaskold
Indexer: Amy Murphy
Cover Designer: Scott Van Atta
Graphic Designer: Anupama Krishnan
Marketing Manager: Sharon Pendergast

20 21 22 23 24 10 9 8 7 6 5 4 3 2

Contents

Foreword

Who is your hero? Growing up you might have identified with Captain America, Aquaman, Superwoman, or a host of other famous heroes. As adults, those characters might have evolved into real-life heroes such as a parent, spouse, student, or mentor. Regardless of who you choose, the characteristics of heroes are similar. Heroes demonstrate compassion, have a strong moral compass, and are brave, selfless, and relentless in the pursuit of achieving what they have been called on to accomplish.

Educators today are modern-day heroes. They wake up every morning with their purpose and moral compass guiding them towards best practices and creative strategies to support the success of all students. As an early learning educator, I saw on a daily basis how much students looked up to their teachers—from the drawings they did during play centers of their teachers as their day-to-day heroes to the expression on their faces when their teacher solved yet another math problem, read a story with enthusiasm, or flew down the slide on the playground with ease. As a secondary principal, I have the honor of serving alongside heroes every day at Ellis Middle School. It could be in the form of Assistant Principal Ryan Barnick (@BarnickRyan), who relentlessly engages and empowers students who have felt like adults have been more like the enemy than the ally in their life. Or it could be in the relentless ways that teams of teachers meet weekly to adjust lessons and curriculum to meet and reach all students they serve. The compassion and care is evident in these middle school superheroes in Austin, Minnesota, even outside of the school when I see these educators at student concerts, sporting events, or even at their students' homes after the funerals of loved ones.

Dr. Ziegler and Dr. Ramage are creating a movement to not only show the importance of hero building in schools but to highlight and share stories of modern-day heroes in our schools and classrooms today. Their work and extensive research is evident in each chapter, and the vision they have for this work is clear, important, and necessary to continue to be the very best for every stakeholder in our school.

Becoming a hero today doesn't require a costume or a superpower. Today's schools are seeking real-life heroes. Our families are looking for selfless leaders ready to advocate for the complex needs, skills, and strengths their children are bringing into school. Our teachers and support staff are looking towards leadership that has a strong purpose, drive, and direction to move the lever towards a positive and productive school climate. And our students, well they deserve an inspirational leader whose vision is large enough that each of them can see a successful version of themselves reflected in it.

By reading this book you are committing to taking the first step to become the hero your school needs you to be. Dr. Ziegler and Dr. Ramage share rationale, strategies, and support to show how to take the qualities of what it means to be a hero and implement them in our schools. Through this journey, you will gain tools, resources, and new powers to guide the path.

The journey starts by finding your moral compass through stories of everyday heroes in our school hallways today. After establishing that foundational core you will learn how to access a deeper call for compassion in leadership and deeper understanding of the why of knowing who we serve on a deeper level. Early on in this book you will have established the why, then Bill and Dave dive right into how to advocate and use these hero building skills to enhance student voice in meaningful ways.

As your journey continues, leading with courage will infuse skills such as innovation and risk-taking in your daily rituals and routines. And while we may be superheroes in the eyes of who we serve, self-care and grace are required to protect us from what lurks in the dark corners in our schools. Fear, frustration, burnout, and secondary trauma fill our halls, and in Chapter Six you will learn ways to build the resilience necessary to lead this work well into the future.

The final part of the journey will be filled with stories of leaders in the field accomplishing this work and ongoing inspiration we all need to be reminded of in our schools today. You will leave this book feeling accomplished, gaining the courage to move forward with the resilience needed to move past obstacles that are placed in your way.

Jessica Cabeen
2017 Minnesota Nationally Distinguished Principal
Principal, Author, and Emerging Hero Builder in
Practice and Action

Preface

"That person who helps others simply because it should or must be done, and because it is the right thing to do, is indeed without a doubt, a real superhero."

—Stan Lee

THE ORIGIN STORY

You don't need superpowers to be a kid's hero; you just need a willing heart, a courageous spirit, and a tireless commitment to excellence. Far too often, leaders are paralyzed by their own fears, shortcomings, or a desire to insist on perfection before moving forward. But your students need you now. The future of our schools depends on our ability to be leaders who nurture and foster heroism in others. This mission does not require supernatural powers. It simply requires a willingness to be intentional in building—among our students, our staff, and within ourselves—heroes who are ready to take on the complex, dynamic, and heroic demands of the future.

There is an intersection between the important work of school leadership and our cultural stories of heroes. Seeing our own students and staff accomplish amazing things and hearing the stories of leaders from around the country fueled our desire to write a book to help leaders create schools that produce heroes. We began to explore parallels between iconic superheroes and the experiences of school leaders. We connect with school leaders on a regular basis, and their successes are legitimate, nonfiction hero stories.

We are showing up for our schools every day, facing many of the same problems, challenges, and demands that you experience. We witness and relish the opportunity to celebrate the victories of student successes that make our work worthwhile. Overwhelmed school leaders often need a boost of inspiration and encouragement to break through the complexity of our work. This book equips leaders to remain inspired and persevere with research-based, relevant, and practical strategies that you can immediately implement in your schools. We hope these stories and tools will inspire leaders to continue your complex calling of building an extraordinary school.

The work we do in schools is unrivaled in importance. Our school settings may not include aliens, superpowers, colorful costumes, or supervillains of the literal kind, or the budget and resources of Marvel Entertainment, but our schools do house real heroes, real struggles, and real victories. This work is for, and about, our students. We see teachers, staff, and school leaders who do the work of heroes. We invite you to unleash your inner hero, to make a difference for your kids by training *them* to be heroes. Our leadership task is to produce students who will change their world for the better.

We want to help you create the culture and climate that produces real heroes. Along the way we will share stories of successes, and occasionally make the connection to some of those wonderful fictitious heroes, so you can be inspired and gain practical ideas to shape your own culture.

THE RATIONALE

Why should you consider the hero building leadership we explore in these pages? Because we believe this book has unique features that other authors have not addressed. As practicing educational leaders, our focus does not dwell on the theoretical but on the practical day-to-day strategies and solutions that will transform your leadership practices. Here are some compelling examples of how this book can help your practice. In these pages, you will find

- Detailed leadership approaches to break through stagnant culture trends for the change your school needs
- Training ideas for your leadership team
- Instruments for reflection to gauge your ongoing progress
- Practical steps for building courage into your leadership practices
- Step-by-step ideas to help you thrive as a leader and navigate the complexities of creating an extraordinary school
- Inspiration presented in a simple, practical, and real-life way
- Hero-building stories from leaders in the field

THE RESULT

Hero-building leadership work will help you look deeply into your school culture and see your students and staff in a fresh and powerful way. It will also force you to look inside and consider your own purpose, calling, and commitment. The goal of our writing is to inspire you to make an even more impactful difference in your school and in the lives of your students and staff. There is no time to hold out for a hero from our community, state department of education, or federal government—we need a hero now! Our students move through our schools too quickly to put off creating the culture and climate they need to reach their full potential. This book is a call to action—a call to remind each of us in school leadership about the responsibility we have to equip ALL students so they can thrive in their unknown future.

OUR JOURNEY TOGETHER

Chapter 1 will set the stage and remind you that being a hero is not painless or easy work, but it is attainable. Take the successes from **Heroes in the Hallways** to your own school. Consider how their inspiring work might influence your own leadership practices. These everyday heroes remind us that leading carries a moral purpose, and it's not just about being a CEO rockstar in an educational setting. We hope you decide to join us in the hero-building leadership journey after reading these authentic successes.

Chapter 2 is an important call to **Look Deep Inside** and see beyond the immediate and obvious. Our students, faculty, and staff all carry an invisible backpack of items to their work and learning. Understanding what fills these backpacks will help us shift the conversation from, "What's wrong with you?" to "What happened to you?" This can make all the difference for a student who struggles before class even gets started. Heroes always have an eye open for those that need extra help; we want to be those heroes.

Heroes all have an origin story that shapes them. We have an origin story, too. In **Chapter 3: True to Life Leadership and Learning,** we try to encourage you to get in touch with your origin—the calling and purpose that brought you into education. We'll look back and consider the myths of learning we've all been told along our journey. School today must be so much more than a mirror of what we did when we went through school 5, 10, or 40 plus years ago!

With all the shouting that's been going on in our world lately, it's important to step back and listen to the important voices that are not routinely included or easily heard. **Chapter 4** shares ideas to **Unleash the Voice and Choice of Students** and really value *and use* student voice in your leadership practices. You will hear about some amazing triumphs and changes in this section that help create real heroes in your school. One of the first ways we can create heroes among our students is to give them a voice.

Are there days when you long to be teleported to another planet filled with eager learners who have no history with our broken, outdated, entrenched, factory-model educational system? If you have these thoughts, **Chapter 5: Lead Like**

an Alien might be your favorite chapter. As a companion to debunking myths, we want to also offer some out-of-this-world thinking to help you move your leadership forward as you build a strong school culture and climate. Even if you find these ideas to be appealing, they take the stamina and courage of a hero to implement for your students.

The leadership journey is a difficult one, and we would be remiss if we did not offer strategies to build resilience and perseverance for you and your students. There are many systems and people in any organization that try to keep the status quo from changing. **Chapter 6: Build Resilience** is meant to encourage you in the work and equip you with ideas to keep moving forward in this important mission. Your students' lives depend on it.

Chapter 7: Go Big or Go Home is filled with inspirational stories and practical strategies to help you make an authentic difference in your classroom, school, district, community, and world. You will gain ideas to help your students make a substantive difference and also feel good about working on a big impact by diligently seeking small impact and building on it. You will see student heroes and hero-building leaders in action.

The book ends with what is arguably the most important leadership trait to pursue. We implore you to **Be Courageous (Chapter 8)** because hero-building leadership work is too important to avoid. The strategies for conducting courageous conversations are among the most important leadership strategies we've ever explored, and practiced, in our own leadership journey. We hope this chapter encourages you to be strong and courageous.

Special Tools

Four of the features we include as tools for extending the learning with the book are Web Resources, Hero SIMs Hero Sightings, and Hero Training. Web resources are mentioned throughout the book and curated at the website mentioned in the description below for your convenience. You will also find a reference to specific simulations in a few key areas of the text. Hero Sighting and Hero Training sections are included at the end of every chapter.

Web Resources: These online extensions to the book are opportunities for resources and sharing. Point your browser to https://www.chaselearning.org/herobuilding to grab digital versions of the reflection tools included throughout the book, share your hero-building successes and stories, or interact with a Hero SIM.

Hero SIM: One hero tool we provide our readers is an opportunity to complete a Hero SIM. This leadership simulation guides readers through a variety of scenarios they can use to strengthen their skills as leaders and challenge their hero leadership muscles. We encourage you to engage in Hero Training with a diverse leadership team.

Hero Sighting: Each chapter includes a section called Hero Sighting. This feature includes reflection questions to guide your work. You can complete this section individually, but we encourage you to work with your leadership team. Hero Sighting cites an aspect of John Hattie's Visible Learning research and places it in the context of the material discussed during the chapter. By using approaches that Hattie has found to be effective in improving learning, we hope to accelerate transformation in your own setting. Hero Sighting is a reminder that we need to make our work visible and actionable.

Hero Training: Each chapter closes with a section called Hero Training. This is an opportunity for you, or you and your whole leadership team, to extend some of the ideas from the chapter to your own leadership practices. Even heroes need to work out, build their muscles, and remain strong and agile. We encourage you to dig into the Hero Training activities, and if you have an alternate training regimen that works well, please let us know so we can share it with other hero leaders. Tweet and tag your ideas by using #HBLschools.

Our Mission

We are grateful for the culture of hero stories that has shaped our thinking about heroes since we were children. Our culture loves these fictional characters! However, we are even more thankful for the real-life educators, leaders, and mentors that influence our thinking about teaching, learning, and leading. These men and women engage with life, including all the challenges and obstacles that must be overcome. They are learners and leaders who inspire others to learn and lead, and so the cycle continues. They change the world for their students. They are the true, real-life heroes for their school.

Aquaman: **"What could be greater than a king?"**

Mera: **"A hero—a king fights for his nation. A hero fights for everyone!"**

Thanks to DC Comics for this powerful reminder. Keep this quote in mind as you read this book, and consider how you can be a fierce and tireless advocate for all kids!

We encourage you to share your own hero stories by using #HBLschools on social media.

Acknowledgments

Bill and Dave want to thank our mentors who spoke, and continue to speak, into our leadership practices. They encourage us to Go Big! We also want to thank the faculty and staff we've had the honor to serve and lead. In those relationships built, mistakes made, ideas implemented, learning shared, and daily grind experienced, we shaped and built culture together. We could not have made a difference in the lives of students without the dedicated staff and faculty at Potts-grove Middle School, Pottsgrove High School, Pottsgrove School District, Pottstown High School, Indian Crest Middle School, and Souderton Area School District. Together we have almost 60 years of serving and leading in K–12 schools, and our successes are built on the work of others who labor with us and beside us.

We've gained so much from working with graduate students in the field of education at several institutions, including California University of Pennsylvania, DeSales University, Drexel University, and Temple University. We are humbled to be in a position to help shape future school leaders during these formative experiences. Many thanks to the professors who share our passion for learning and leading and freely share their insights, struggles, and successes with us.

We would be remiss if we failed to dedicate this book to the people we want to empower most—our students. A teacher and a student share a strong bond, and we each remember students who have shaped our lives in profound ways. We marveled at their amazing grit to overcome tremendous difficulties or witnessed the tragic circumstances that shortened their opportunity to shine. A school leader has the opportunity, and privilege, to see some things that a teacher may never see about a student's world beyond the school walls. In these heartbreaking moments of pain, or exuberant moments of triumph and success, we say thank you to the students and families who have trusted us to be hero-building leaders.

We're still learning and can't wait to see what lies in store as we continue to support and launch students into a future where they will excel and create the innovations that keep us all moving ahead successfully. Nurturing culture is work that is continuous and constantly rewarding. We hope this book, and the stories of hero-building leaders, will encourage you to press on in this important work of culture building that leads to real-life heroes.

PUBLISHER'S ACKNOWLEDGMENTS

Corwin gratefully acknowledges the contributions of the following reviewers:

Jessica Cabeen
Principal
Austin, MN

Carrie Carpenter
Reading Specialist, Oregon Teacher of the Year 2003
Redmond, OR

Lisa Graham
Director, Early Childhood Education
Castle Rock, CO

Jessica Johnson
Principal/District Assessment Coordinator, Author
Juneau, WI

About the Authors

Dr. Bill Ziegler is the proud principal of Pottsgrove High School in Pennsylvania, the school he attended as a student. Dr. Ziegler is an award-winning school leader, author, and speaker. Dr. Ziegler is an Apple Distinguished Educator, a member of the Apple Distinguished Schools Advisory Board, and a member of the Board of Directors for the National Association of Secondary School Principals. He has been recognized as the 2016 Pennsylvania Principal of the Year and the 2015 National Association of Secondary School Principals (NASSP) Digital Principal Award Winner. Dr. Ziegler was honored to be the president of the Pennsylvania Principals Association in 2013 and 2015. He is the coauthor of the Corwin book *Future Focused Leaders: Relate, Innovate, and Invigorate for Real Educational Change*. Bill also served on a team from NASSP that authored the Building Ranks Framework for school leaders. Dr. Ziegler served as the closing keynote at the National Principals Conference, and he is a highly sought after consultant to speak around the country on school leadership, school culture, trauma, future-ready learning, digital integration, and many other topics.

Dr. Ziegler is the owner of Chase Learning, a professional educational consulting company serving educational leaders, school districts, and principal organizations. Bill was selected to serve on the USA Team of School Leaders who spent a month in China providing professional learning to over 4,000 Chinese principals. Dr. Ziegler earned his doctorate at Temple University where he currently serves as an adjunct professor in the department of education. Check out Dr. Ziegler's podcast for school leaders entitled *Lead the Way, a Podcast for School Leaders*. Dr. Ziegler has served over 26 years in education as a high school social studies teacher, high school assistant principal, middle school principal, and in his current role of high school principal.

Bill resides in Pennsylvania with his wife and two children. Bill can often be found traveling with his family, dropping a line in a lake, off roading with his Jeep, playing the sax in church, or cheering on his favorite Philly sports teams. Twitter: @DrBill Ziegler

Dave Ramage, PhD has been a public school educator for more than 30 years as a junior high music teacher, K–12 instructional coach, middle school assistant principal, and middle school principal. He currently serves as the Director of Integration for Learning and Instruction at Pottsgrove School District. Dave has also done graduate level teaching for several universities, and enjoys supporting doctoral students.

Dave is the co-author of the Corwin book, *Future Focused Leaders: Relate, Innovate and Invigorate for Real Educational Change.* He was a national finalist in the Technology Leaders award sponsored by Technology & Learning magazine. He has presented at regional and national conferences including PETE&C, NECC, PASCD, ISTE, and the National Principals Conference.

Dave is honored to be an Apple Distinguished Educator and eagerly looks for ways to help schools use technology to enhance and expand the ways we approach learning. He supports the Apple Distinguished schools in Pottsgrove and welcomes the visitors who travel to see our staff, students, principals, and administrators in action. Stories of student successes always trace their roots to strong relationships and Dr. Ramage is humbled and blessed to be a partner in the vital work of hero building to transform school culture.

Dave loves to make music, especially while playing the electric bass. When road conditions permit you'll find him on two wheels carving up some of the great roads in our area. Dave and his wife live in Pennsylvania. Their three children are doing some pretty heroic teaching and learning where they are planted. Twitter: @DrDaveRamage

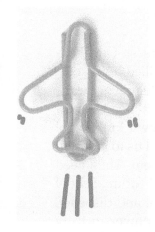

HEROES IN THE HALLWAYS

"A hero is no braver than an ordinary man, but he is brave five minutes longer."

—Ralph Waldo Emerson

R alph Waldo Emerson suggests a hero is no braver than any ordinary man or woman, it's just that they are brave for "five minutes longer." Who is your hero? Maybe it's your parent, a teacher, spouse, child, or someone you know who overcame insurmountable odds. The best heroes are not the ones in comic books or movies leaping over tall buildings or flying into outer space. The best heroes are people that we see, know, and trust. The real people who do extraordinary things, or perhaps they do ordinary things in ways that consistently honor and serve others over time. Teachers who regularly give all they have for their students are heroes. School leaders will quickly stand and applaud teachers as heroes, but these same leaders are reluctant to call their own work heroic. We believe teachers, staff members, school leaders, and students can all

> The best heroes are people who we see, know, and trust.
>
> @DrBillZiegler @DrDaveRamage

be real heroes. Our hallways are filled with current and potential heroes!

We don't need superpowers to be a kid's hero! What we need is to be there for them. Kids need us to invest in them, come alongside them, and empower them. They need to know that we care for their well-being and future. School leaders often get sucked into a vortex of doubt and disbelief, fearing that they don't have the ability and power to truly move a school forward and make a difference in the life of a kid. Just the opposite is true! Our schools and kids are going to be successful if we commit to being hero building leaders dedicated to preparing kids for their unknown future.

We don't see exemplary school leaders as heroes who are superhuman and therefore faultless, immune to pain and failure, or inaccessible to others. Just the opposite, they are highly relational, focused on servant leadership, resilient, fierce, relentless, and tireless advocates for kids. These advocates for kids and staff are the heroes who are making real, sustainable, and positive change for their schools. It's leaders like this who we seek to empower, encourage, and inspire with this book so that they can continue the great work of hero building and leadership in their schools.

Hero-building leadership is dependent on collaborative leadership. It's not about one leader driving the school forward but rather a collaborative focus of leaders committed to the mission of building heroes. Hero builders are leaders who understand that collaboration is key to success, the foundation of growth, and the heartbeat of progress for the work of creating hero students who will change the world. In *Collaborative Leadership* (2017), Peter DeWitt writes, "Collaborative leadership includes the purposeful actions we take as leaders to enhance the instruction of teachers, build deep relationships with all stakeholders, and deepen our learning together." It's this type of leadership that hero-building leadership strives to build on and nurture. Faculty, staff, students, parents, and other adults who engage in hero-building leadership nurture, develop, and build students who are the heroes for their community, region, and the world. Our students are the young heroes who will transform our world and serve to bring about positive change for generations. We passionately believe that if the schools don't get things right, the world never will.

You Don't Need Superpowers to Be a Kid's Hero is written to inspire extraordinary school leaders who equip and empower their students and staff to do amazing things. This chapter will tell the stories of school leaders doing heroic things for students. These heroes in the hallways are daily making a difference in the lives of students and staff. They are working tirelessly to be advocates for kids, to innovate learning, to strengthen community partnerships, and to make the tough and courageous decisions to move their schools, learning, and students forward.

> *You Don't Need Superpowers to Be a Kid's Hero* is written to inspire extraordinary school leaders who equip and empower their students and staff to do amazing things.
>
> @DrBillZiegler @DrDaveRamage

These stories span the country and include elementary school, middle school, and high school from urban, rural, and suburban settings that include students as diverse as the communities represented. They feature leaders who are advocating for kids in a way that empowers and inspires. We hope you will enjoy reading the stories of these school leaders, be encouraged by their work, equipped by the strategies they're using, and inspired to continue doing amazing things for your students, staff, and community.

All of these leaders would humbly say they are just showing up every day to do what's best for kids. If you were to ask their students, parents, or staff, they would say they have a real hero in their school's hallway. As you read their stories, it may remind you of a real hero who influenced you. Their leadership may be a significant factor in your calling to make a difference as a school leader yourself.

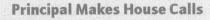

Principal Makes House Calls

Principal, Mr. Matthew Moyer—Rupert Elementary School, Pottstown, PA

Twitter: @MoyerMatthewD @PrincipalsofL

I'MPACT Program Makes House Calls

(385 students in preK through Grade 4: 74 percent economically disadvantaged; Demographics: 34.2 percent White, 33.4 percent African-American, 17.6 percent Hispanic, 12.6 percent multiracial, 1 percent Asian, 1 percent other)

Our first school leader sheds light on the importance of looking deep inside and seeing what students and staff bring to school by connecting with students and families in their lives beyond school. This leader values and understands the importance of understanding the invisible backpack and helping faculty and staff gain an understanding of the lives our students lead and how their lives affect the ways we learn and relate together. Learn more about the invisible backpack and looking deep in Chapter 2.

Imagine being an elementary school student at home watching your favorite cartoon or playing ball with your sister when a knock comes at the door. Your parents answer the door, and it's your school principal and teachers. Principal Moyer and Rupert teachers visit students at their homes as part of their school district's home visitation program called I'MPACT (I'M Pottstown Action Community Team).

Principal Moyer and his faculty/staff members wanted to recognize the kids in school who weren't getting recognized for whatever reason.

"The team visited students from prekindergarten to fourth grade to congratulate them and their families and to acknowledge the students' success during the first marking period. The program's mission is to 'celebrate learning.' It develops positive communications between the school and families by building relationships with community members. The team makes door-to-door visits to surprise students and their families with certificates of achievement and I'MPACT winner shirts. Students are congratulated for their hard work, citizenship, and positive behavior." The I'MPACT team consists of teachers, support staff, parents, and administrators from Rupert Elementary School.

Principal Moyer said, "This is a tremendous program that allows us to not only recognize positive behaviors in our students but gives our staff the opportunity to meet students and parents outside of the school building in an environment that is conducive to promoting positive relationships.

As I look at these youngsters that we are recognizing, it reminds me that they are the reason we say 'Proud to be from Pottstown.'" (Brandt, 2014)

Principal Moyer shared, "Each grade level selects one student. We try to select the children who don't normally get recognized, like children who had a lot of improvement in some area. We strive to recognize the kids that always work hard and give their best."

In a neighboring school district, a retired elementary principal would visit the homes of each kindergarten student to welcome them to the school, meet their parents, and read them a story from a book. Dr. Ron Christman served as the principal of Gilbertsville Elementary School in the Boyertown School District. He had close to 200 kindergarten students who he scheduled these home visits with. At the end of his visits, he would give the students the book. Even years later, there are students in the community who still have that children's book on their bookshelves and an eternal memory of a principal who left an indelible mark on their young lives and the start of their education.

It's principals like Matt Moyer and Ron Christman who are going the extra mile for their students, and they are advocating for kids through their actions. Principal Moyer and Christman understand the need to look deep inside the hearts and minds of kids to help them be successful in school. In Chapter 2, we dive deeper into how school leaders can do this and share how to support and help students who are experiencing trauma, how to connect and see all students in the school, and how to develop the hidden strengths of children. Plus, we will share how to nurture and build a culture of relationships, resources, interventions, and wisdom.

Manufacturing Our Future

Principal Darci Pollard

Twitter: @ACSCougars

Andrew Carnegie Elementary School

(631 Students: 82 percent economically disadvantaged; Demographics: 97.8 percent African-American, 1.4 percent Hispanic, and 0.8 percent other)

This courageous leader was not satisfied to perpetuate the belief that the information economy was beyond the reach of her female students.

(Continued)

(Continued)

Her leadership created a space where students could not only gain skills for coding and computer science, but also where they cultivated attitudes and habits that reminded them to break through glass ceilings and barriers. The "Black Girls Code" club was a community of learners dedicated to learning resilience and building grit. We talk more about how hero-building leaders create these kinds of opportunities for their students in Chapter 6.

Principal Darci Pollard and her staff are committed to engaging students through the use of technology. They understand the power technology has to equip and empower students for the future. Their school is equipped with Chromebooks, but Darci and her team didn't believe they were using them to their fullest potential. They were searching for ways to engage all students, especially their girls, in coding. Darci and her faculty believe that coding is the language of the future and that the students of Andrew Carnegie Elementary School need to know and understand the basics of coding.

In an effort to engage girls with coding, Principal Pollard and her faculty started a club called, "Black Girls Code." This club became a huge hit with girls, and they signed up to learn coding in a fun and engaging way. The girls use Ozobots, which are small robots to teach coding and creativity. They also use Scratch coding, which is a programming language and online community where children can code and program through the power of stories, games, and animation. Scratch builds creativity, collaboration, and systems thinking through a fun and interactive digital tool for students.

Now, the Black Girls Code club is hosting a family STEM (science, technology, engineering, and mathematics) night for families to learn what the girls and school are doing around STEM and technology. Students of the Black Girls Code club searched out funding for the event and worked to plan the STEM night for parents.

Black Girls Code is an organization based out of San Francisco that has the mission to increase the number of women of color in the digital space by empowering girls of color ages seven to seventeen to become innovators in STEM fields, leaders in their communities, and builders of their futures through exposure to computer science and technology.

Principal Pollard partnered with the University of Chicago, UChicago STEM Education Program, to build the Black Girls Code club. By doing this, she was able to get university volunteers and students to help out, had access to university technology, and it provided the girls with role models who were coding as college students.

Principal Pollard shared, "The Black Girls Code club has been great for our school. Girls are now empowered to learn coding. Most importantly, they are learning leadership, creativity, problem solving, and collaboration. I'm so proud of our girls and all they have done to strengthen their learning."

Principal Pollard and her team are modeling the practices showcased in Chapter 7: "Go Big or Go Home! Empowering Students to Be Global Game Changers." The girls at Andrew Carnegie Elementary School are global game changers in their school and community.

We commend Principal Pollard and her team for courageously breaking down historical barricades to engage students in learning. She understands that it will take alien and out-of-this-world ideas to challenge and shatter the status quo for her students to grow, lead, and learn. Learn more about breaking down historical barricades to learning, thinking differently as a school leader, and training as a hero in upcoming chapters.

Telling Your School's Story

Principal Boomer Kennedy

Twitter: @BoomerKennedy

Forbush High School

School Twitter: @ForbushHS, Forbush, NC

(923 students in Grades 8 through 12: 37 percent economically disadvantaged; Demographics: 78 percent White, 18 percent Hispanic, 3 percent African-American, 1 percent other)

Boomer's story reminds us that it's okay—even necessary—to venture into territory we have not mastered in order to help our students and staff. Frequently, leaders feel the pressure to only lead in areas where

(Continued)

(Continued)

they are considered to be experts. Boomer (and Bill and Dave) knows this superhero CEO-saves-the-day mentality is not what we need in our schools. If we want our students to believe failure is a part of learning, and we all keep learning, we need to take steps like Boomer did. He saw an authentic need to tell his school's story, and he took the risk to make it happen. Find more information about taking leadership risks in Chapter 8.

Boomer Kennedy and his team understand the importance of leveraging social media to tell their school's story. Even as a young principal, Kennedy doesn't consider himself a techie or digital leader, he came late to the game regarding social media. He learned and grew in this area because he saw the power of social media to showcase the work of his students and staff. He realized one of the most powerful tools to brand his school and to tell his school's story required him to jump into social media headfirst.

Principal Kennedy shared his journey of growing in digital storytelling to tell his school's story in a recent article from the Chase Learning blog. In the following text, he provides insights into his journey:

"My colleagues may find this surprising, since I am pretty active on Twitter now, but I was not one of the first people to jump onto the 'social media' bandwagon. I never got into Facebook, and I was slow to show interest in Twitter, Instagram, or Snapchat. However, social media is a powerful tool that schools, principals, and teachers should be utilizing. If you are not, you are missing out on opportunities to promote your school, communicate with your stakeholders, and grow as a professional.

First, social media tools are a great way to communicate with parents and students on a regular basis. Announcements, special events, upcoming activities, and even weather updates can be shared immediately using any social media platform. Social media is also a great way to 'show off' your school and the accomplishments of your students. My assistant principals and I manage our school's Twitter account, which is also linked to our Facebook account. We try to post and retweet sports scores, classroom activities, club ceremonies, and other student accomplishments throughout the week. This is a great way for your school to 'tell its story' while also boosting school and community pride. Many students and parents are using these platforms, so it only makes sense for schools to meet them where they are. I highly recommend a free app called 'Buffer' that allows you to schedule posts days, or even weeks, in advance. Buffer is compatible with Facebook, Twitter, and Instagram, making it easy to link multiple accounts so that you save time while reaching an even larger audience.

Lastly, I highly recommend that teachers and principals use social media platforms to connect with fellow educators. Twitter is a great avenue for sharing ideas with educators from around the world. There are so many great blog posts and articles that are shared on Twitter and other social media platforms; it's like free professional development for teachers and principals! Moreover, it is important for our students to see appropriate social media usage. Many of our students do not know how to maturely participate in an online community, so it is vital that we, as educators, utilize these platforms in a manner that models responsible digital citizenship. Sharing articles and ideas, encouraging meaningful dialogue, promoting our schools, communicating upcoming events, and showing off the accomplishments of our students is a powerful way to do just that."

Boomer Kennedy

Boomer shares a powerful reminder to us all on how we need to continue to grow and develop our skills to further the work of our students, staff, and school. He couldn't let his fears or insecurities get in the way of showcasing the awesome work of his students and staff. He was courageous enough to learn something new, to admit that he needed to grow, and to take action to improve in this area.

Boomer understands the importance of showcasing student and staff voice and choice that is discussed deeper in Chapter 4. In Chapter 4, we provide school leaders with examples on how to enhance their school's ability to listen to student voice and to increase student choice opportunities in the school. Mr. Kennedy also understands the need to lead courageously by admitting that he needs help and taking the necessary steps to improve as a leader. We discuss this deeper in Chapter 8: "Be Courageous: Risking It All for What's Right." In Chapter 8, readers learn how to lead with courageous fortitude, the power of authenticity, the need to ask for help, and the skills to have courageous conversations in order to transform your school.

Leading by Example

Principal Darrell Webb

Twitter: @DocWebb1911

Turner Elementary School in Caddo Parish School District, Shreveport, LA

School Twitter: @tigerpride2017

(1,063 students: 92 percent economically disadvantaged; Demographics: 87 percent African-American, 5.9 percent Hispanic, 5.0 percent White, 2.1 percent other)

Darrell's story touches on several aspects of hero-building leadership that create value for his students and staff. You can read more about unleashing the voice and choice of students in Chapter 4 and learn to build resilience and grit for your students in Chapter 6. Darrell's story is all about the authentic, vulnerable, true-to-life leadership of serving others that we discuss in Chapter 3. His unconventional, out-of-this-world approach is an idea we explore in Chapter 5.

Darrell Webb is an innovative leader who understands the importance of leading by example. He models what he expects from his staff, and he works to build trust with everyone in his school. Darrell understands that leadership is more than just a title, it's a consistent and persistent focus on servant leadership committed to the success of every kid in his school. This school year, his team created a welcome video for students entitled, "This Is the Year." The video show students and staff working together to make this the best year ever. Visit our website to view the video at www.chaselearning.org/herobuilding. This video is one testimony of his school's dedication to the success of every child and an example of Darrell's leadership, which is focused on leading by example.

Principal Webb shares, "A leader without a vision is like a car with no wheels; you won't get very far." Any successful leader led with and was able to communicate his or her vision. According to Maxwell, "People buy into the leader before they buy into the vision." I have experienced this greatly in my first years in leadership. For my first year as principal, a few teachers bought into my vision from my communication of the vision and from what they knew about me in general. It wasn't until my third year that I began to see a stronger investment into my vision from my stakeholders. It took proving myself to my staff and getting them to buy into me first. I feel a large contribution of this buy-in was due to me leading by example. I am the first on campus and many days the last to leave the campus. I expect my staff to be on time, so I am always on time. I report to duty every morning and afternoon as well as during lunch. I teach lessons, watch classes for teachers, work weekends with teachers, change trash can liners, serve food in the cafeteria, and eat with teachers/staff. I even performed my first dance in front of an audience for my staff and students. I spend about 15 percent of my day in my office. As a leader, you have to be visible and relevant to your staff and be approachable and positive. We all know the saying, "When momma ain't happy, nobody happy"; well that same saying applies to the school principal. As a school leader, we set the tone for the school. To want a positive staff who has fun with the students, we as leaders have to be positive and fun to work with first. I want a leader who is out here with me in the trenches and not afraid to get his or her hands dirty. As a school leader, we have to be humble and serve in the same trenches we are leading.

Culture Wins Out!

Principal Mariah Rackley (2018 NASSP Digital Award Winner)

Twitter @MrsRackleyCCMS

Cedar Crest Middle School, Lebanon, PA

(1,150 students: 38.4 percent economically disadvantaged; Demographics: 80 percent White, 12 percent Hispanic, 4 percent African-American, 2 percent multiracial, 1 percent Asian, 1 percent other)

Principal Rackley understands a school can't move forward without a healthy, positive, and collaborative focus on what's best for kids. She understands one of the best ways to value students is to listen to them. Hopefully we can all recall a time when we felt that we were truly heard and understood. What a powerful experience. Mariah's hero-building leadership is helping to create a culture where students are heard, and

(Continued)

(Continued)

their ideas are brought to life. Enjoy her story, and learn about more ways to unleash the voice, choice, and agency of students in Chapter 4.

When asked to share about school culture and how she is working with her staff to nurture a positive, caring, and student-centered school culture, Principal Rackley provided the following response:

"Culture is a crucial part of our job as administrators. It has to be at the core of all that we do while being fostered and cultivated. Culture does not happen by accident. It takes commitment, vision, and dedication to a common goal and belief system. Leaders have to model our expectations for our staff. Kindness, respect, compassion, humanity, positivity, risk-taking, grace . . . our students and staff become a reflection of those fundamental values that shape our culture.

We strive to provide a student-centered culture that is safe and supportive where we celebrate success, risk taking, and innovation. We have high expectations for student achievement and staff performance. We recognize the importance of a growth mindset to constantly improve our practice and think differently about how we 'do school.' Most importantly, we keep our focus on our STUDENTS—in every decision.

Over the past few years, I have become a firm believer in student agency, but it is an incredible paradigm shift. If you have established a culture that values student success and encourages risk taking and individual pursuit of skills, interests, and aptitudes, then choice is a next logical step. Whether you call it student agency, student voice, or student choice, the foundational concept is the same—taking advantage of student interests to make learning meaningful and relevant.

Think about how we, as leaders, engage in activities and projects differently when we are interested, motivated, and invested in topics that are personally significant and relevant! What if we give students the opportunity to learn in ways that are meaningful and make sense to them? What if we allow staff to select professional development topics that connect to their passions and their teaching assignments?

In our school, we have created a community service/outreach opportunity for all of our students and staff members called Falcons CARE (Cooperation and Respect for Everyone). Our groups are student selected based on common interests, beliefs, passions, and sparks. It is a time of connection, community, teamwork, citizenship, and thoughtfulness about the 'greater good' that exists outside of Cedar Crest Middle School. Our groups work with community groups like local nursing homes, animal shelters, our Mini-THON committee, and Domestic Violence Intervention (DVI), to name a few. Our students take on projects like landscaping our campus, quilting for DVI, canning for Mini-THON, and supporting our military. We educate our students about service animal organizations, healthy relationships, childhood cancer and its impact on families, and so much more! Our students learn tolerance, acceptance, compassion, and kindness. We teach our students how to make a difference in our world. They gain insight to the most important life lessons of valuing people as individuals and understanding humanity.

Success breeds success! Students and staff connecting over common interests, experiences, and passions improves your culture. A thriving, positive culture where students and staff are encouraged to grow and take risks inspires high achievement and student success. Connections to other people build an environment where people feel safe. When students and staff feel empowered to take risks, innovate, create, and explore new learning, academic success soars! When students are achieving at high levels in a student-centered environment where LEARNING is the priority, the culture blossoms into a place where students and staff want to learn, work, create, innovate, excel, and succeed together. Connections, culture, choice . . . they are interrelated in an intricate dance that evolves as the goals in each of the three areas are realized.

At the end of the day, I have learned that the most meaningful lessons we teach our students do not come from textbooks. The most important things students learn are those lessons we model—how to be kind to others, how to care for each other, how to be members of a community, how to respect others, how to be a good citizen. I hope students and families leave Cedar Crest Middle School confident that we helped them to be better people, better humans. Our students will change our world—we hope our influence makes their impact a positive one!"

Mariah Rackley

Just like the other principals featured in this chapter, Mariah doesn't consider what she is doing as anything heroic. She's doing what she believes is best for kids, this is exactly what a hero-building school leader does.

Mariah's story probably inspired you to consider ways to improve the culture and climate of your school. Read more about unleashing student voice and choice in Chapter 4 and true-to-life leadership in Chapter 3.

Authentic Leadership

Megan Black, Assistant Principal

Twitter: @MaBlackOW

Olathe High School, Olathe, KS

(2,413 students in Grades 9 through12: 32 percent economically disadvantaged; Demographics: 55 percent White, 24 percent Hispanic, 12 percent African-American, 4 percent Asian, 4 percent multiracial, 1 percent other)

Megan reminds us that hero-building leadership principles are timeless. As generations of new leaders emerge, and seasoned leaders step away, we share the passion and responsibility of creating the best spaces for our students' success that we can. This is the work for everyone in the school, and Megan offers some great reminders for ways to create this powerful culture for our students. See how John Wooden's work connects to our schools, and how this young leader has set a true-to-life example we can all learn from. Read more about authentic leading in Chapter 3.

Megan Black is a young school leader focused on growing and learning. She loves her work at Olathe High School and understands the need for authenticity as a school leader. Veteran school leaders can learn a lot from this millennial school leader—we certainly have! Her passion, authenticity, and focus on working hard is admirable. Assistant Principal Black has grit, and she is willing to do whatever it takes to lead students to success. Megan shares two lessons that she learned about authentic leadership that is committed to working hard for kids. Below are excerpts from Megan Black's recent blog post for the Chase Learning blog:

We millennials get a bad rap for our lack of authenticity, as many people don't perceive us as genuine. Starting in college, my leadership role model has been John Wooden. So, ironically, I'm taking my cues from one of the greatest, most authentic leaders, born in 1910. Each lesson is a quote from Wooden, and I'll elaborate on what they mean to me as a school leader.

Lesson 1: Nothing will work unless you do.

This is a lesson that my parents taught me very early on in my life. If you're not willing to work hard and better yourself every day at the things in which you strive to be successful, then don't be surprised when you fall short. As a school leader, it is important that teachers can expect that you will work as hard as you can on the things in your charge. Part of being an authentic leader is being a person willing to take any challenges head on. This can present itself in many different forms, especially depending on your role in your school. In our building, each assistant principal has distinct responsibilities. Mine come in the form of curriculum and instruction. Each member of our admin team puts in hours and hours of hard work specific to their responsibilities. We value hard work, and we don't stop until the job is done. I love that about our team. For me, hard work looks like:

- Collaborating with teachers on mission, vision, and goals
- Providing top-notch, personalized professional development
- Learning as much as I can, as often as I can
- Providing resources and feedback to teachers

Lesson 2: Things turn out best for the people who make the best of the way things turn out.

This is one of my favorite quotes by Coach Wooden. It's his way of saying, "When life hands you lemons, make lemonade." Every single day, we are faced with stressful situations. Every single day, we could let that stress bog us down and start to make us truly unhappy, and nobody wants to work for an unhappy leader. As administrators, we see students who really struggle. It may be behavior, academics, mental health, a trauma-filled student, or any combination of the above. We also navigate stressful situations with other adults in the building and work to find resolution for all. There are days when you get to your desk at 4:00 pm and feel truly beaten down. We've all been there. But, if at the end of the day, you know in your heart that you did well by students and staff in the building, things have a way of working out. Now, back to Lesson 1—things don't necessarily "work themselves out." They work out because of the hard work we put into each situation in our care. Here are the biggest takeaways from this lesson:

- Keep a positive outlook, there is always a way to successfully navigate through a given situation. Your positivity has to be genuine, or people will see right through it.

(Continued)

(Continued)

- Reflection is key. If you feel like you didn't make the best out of a situation, change your actions for next time. The most authentic leaders are the ones who learn from mistakes.

As a young leader, I hope to make it clear to students and staff that I genuinely care about them as people and that I will work hard day in and day out to see through our mission. It's important as a young leader to focus on values that transcend generations. The things I mentioned: hard work, making the best out of any situation, and genuinely listening to others, even those who disagree; I hope they speak to a leader of any age.

Megan Black

If you asked Megan if she was a hero, she would say that she is too young or that she's just doing what she thinks is best for kids. But, this talented millennial is wise beyond her years and practicing hero-building leadership on a daily basis. The students at Olathe are blessed to have her as their assistant principal.

HEROES ARE BUILT

Heroes are built, not born. Being a hero takes a conscious and intentional focus on committing to something higher than yourself. It requires you to put aside your own wants, sacrifice for the greater good, and have a tireless commitment to improving the lives of others. We are not calling school leaders to some fictitious and unreachable level of leadership; just the opposite. We challenge you to live out the words of this book and to work every day to be a focused, tireless, and vocal advocate for kids. By doing this, you are working on hero-building leadership that will create an extraordinary school for your students. It's close to impossible to be committed to hero-building leadership and not have your school become an extraordinary school. Schools reflect their leaders. If the leaders in the school are dedicated to hero-building leadership then the lives of students and everyone in the school will be strengthened. Our kids, and our schools, are hungering for leaders who are committed to hero-building leadership.

The culture of hero-building leadership is collaborative at its core, we cannot do this work alone. Be intentional in building a team, schedule collaborative leadership time, and commit to doing this work together.

Hero-building leadership nurtures a school culture that values everyone, is committed to success of all members of the school culture, and strives to challenge everyone to fulfill their dreams and aspirations. This type of culture needs intentional leadership and focus to maintain a steady level of growth and nurturing.

Hero-building leadership is meant for all leaders, not just the principal team. Teachers, school counselors, para-educators, and all additional support-

> The culture of hero-building leadership is collaborative at its core—we cannot do this work alone.
>
> @DrBillZiegler @DrDaveRamage

ing staff are encouraged to read this book and practice hero-building leadership principles. We encourage you to work together as a diverse school leadership team to complete the Hero Training at the end of each chapter. If you really want to take your hero-building leadership to the next level, consider having a collaborative book study with students and work through the Hero Training activities at the end of each chapter with students, staff, and parents.

We close out this chapter with a powerful quote from one of our favorite poets, Maya Angelou. Let this quote challenge all of us to be heroes who focus on making sure every child feels valued, encouraged, and empowered.

"I've learned that people will forget what you said, people will forget what you did, but people will never forget how you made them feel."

—Maya Angelou

HERO SIGHTING

"Actively working towards developing positive teacher–student relationships becomes a primary goal, one that establishes your professional standing, and allows you to have a strong effect on the lives of your students" (Hattie & Yates, 2014, p.19).

Reflect with your team. What stories about creating relationships can you share? What impact have you and your staff had on the lives of the students you serve?

Take some time to consider a powerful story that describes the impact you or a colleague has had with one of your school's students. Try to condense this story into a short video, podcast, or written piece that can be shared (or read) in three minutes or less. Creating a collection of these stories helps others see what heroes look like in the school setting and reinforces the culture of hero-building that will transform your school.

HERO TRAINING

Use these activities to nurture your skills. Even better—gather with your team to embed these skills in your work and empower your students to become heroes that change their world.

Hero Training for this chapter is all about telling your story. This kind of exercise can be a powerful type of professional learning (Ramage, 2007). It also provides powerful material to explore beliefs and communicate with a wide range of stakeholders.

1. Work with your team to create and write your school's story. Write the story in 250 words or less, and then share it out with everyone in your school.
2. Who are the heroes in your school? Take time to celebrate them and elevate them for the work that they are doing on a daily basis.

3. Host a superhero day in your school by encouraging everyone to wear their favorite superhero outfits and celebrate the work of the student and staff heroes in your school.
4. Showcase your school's story in a Tweet.
5. Create a one-minute video that features your school story, and post it on social media like Instagram, FB, or Twitter. Be sure to include #HBLschools.
6. Work with your team to draw a picture that represents your school's story. Share the picture with your students, staff, and on social media.
7. Do a storyboard or comic book style version of your story by capturing the key elements with simple visuals. Use your storyboard to inform your other story formats.

Visit our website at **www.chaselearning.org/herobuilding** to view videos of Heroes in our Hallways—Examples of School Leaders and what they are doing.

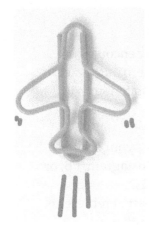

LOOK DEEP INSIDE

See What Students and Staff Really Bring to School

*"There is looking, and there is seeing. When we are looking,
we are not seeing."*

—Umair Haque

In addition to the hero-building leadership stories you read in Chapter 1, we offer an example from Bill's early years in the classroom. See how his perception about a student was dramatically altered as their relationship grew. The first impression was not really the full story. See what unfolded.

Alfonz sat in the first row, second seat back in my twelfth-grade American Government class. Every day, Alfonz would come into class tired and exhausted. He would regularly fall asleep in my class, and I would do my best to wake him up and engage him in the lesson. Alfonz was a nice young man who appeared to have little interest in school and seemed somewhat disconnected from his peers. It took Alfonz all he had to get his work done in class, and he barely did any homework. I worked with Alfonz, offered to stay after school to tutor him, and adjusted his homework schedule to support him, but all of these efforts fell short in motivating him in the class. He would occasionally jump into a conversation or debate, and when he did, wow, did he have a ton to contribute. His smile lit up the room, and his thoughts challenged us to think. But these bursts of energy and engagement were sporadic and short lived. I could tell Alfonz was a smart young man and one that had a bright future, but we needed to identify what was holding him back.

Alfonz benefited directly from the hero leadership that started the I'MPACT initiative we highlighted in Chapter 1. It was around 8:00 p.m. on a winter night when the team walked up the steps to his house. As the team knocked on the door, they could hear small children running around and having fun in the house. It was a lively house, filled with smiles and fun activity. Alfonz greeted us at the door and invited us into his home. We asked to meet Alfonz's parents, and he said his mom was working all night. We discovered his dad wasn't in the picture at all. There stood Alfonz, the oldest of four, supervising his three younger siblings. Alfonz was making dinner at the time and kindly asked us to join in on the family meal. We asked Alfonz how often he had to run the family like he was doing. His response broke our hearts. "I do this every night," he shared. "I do the wash, make the meals, pack lunches for the next day, get my brother and sisters ready for school, and I put them to bed." He shared how his mom works the evening shift to pay the bills and to keep the house running. His mom is a wonderful woman who was doing everything she could to help her kids have a good life. Without her working, the family would have lost the house, so Alfonz took it upon himself to be the parent of the house when his mom was working. As a young teen, Alfonz had more responsibility in life than most of the I'MPACT members.

As we walked back down the steps out of Alfonz's house and down the sidewalk, tears started to run down my face as I realized why he was falling asleep in my class every day. He worked his tail off each night and went to bed late every night because he was helping his brothers, sisters, and mom. I felt guilty about how I considered him a lazy kid who probably stayed up late playing video games or watching television. The visit to Alfonz's house gave me an entirely new perspective on Alfonz and why he was falling asleep in my class.

What are students coming to school with every day that you have no clue about? What are they hiding in their invisible backpacks?

THE INVISIBLE BACKPACK

Lydia Knier, 7th grade student

Hopeworks, an organization based in Camden, New Jersey, has been working with our schools, and they use a term that really resonates with our experiences as school leaders working with a wide variety of students. That term is "the invisible backpack." As stated on their website, the mission of Hopeworks is "Hopeworks 'N Camden uses education, technology and entrepreneurship to partner with young men and women as they identify and earn a sustainable future. Together we seize the opportunity to heal and thrive in the midst of violence and poverty" (Hopeworks, 2017).

Have you ever watched kids carry backpacks? Some of them fill the bags so full that it looks like the bags are going to pull them down while they are walking. Their backpacks are filled with textbooks, notebooks, pens, pencils, gum, gym clothes, their lunch bags, and so much more. But just like the bookbags we can see filled to the max with school stuff, their invisible backpacks that they bring to school every day are weighing them down even more. These backpacks are leaving the scars of more than just a sore back. The traumatic experiences students carry from their childhood are still brought to school every day in their invisible backpack. These experiences can easily entangle them and hold them back from learning, growing, and flourishing as students and young adults. According to a study from the Centers for Disease Control and Prevention, childhood trauma is more widespread than many have thought, and it's often not invisible (1998). The National Child Traumatic Stress Network shares that one out of every four children attending school has been exposed to a traumatic event that can affect learning and/or behavior (NCTSN Child Trauma Toolkit for Educators, 2008).

Bruce Banner is an Ivy League graduate and a renowned scientist. Dr. Banner conducted research on radioactive materials and gamma radiation. He is a mild-mannered, soft-spoken intellectual man who is eager to learn and conduct research. But, Bruce carries a secret worry and pain of embarrassment with him everywhere he goes. Other people can't see this traumatic event until he becomes distressed, injured, or angry. Bruce tries to fight off the transformation that takes place in his life when he faces stress or pain, but he is overpowered, and the stress turns him into someone entirely different than the mild-mannered and soft-spoken researcher he tries to remain.

Bruce Banner turns into the Incredible Hulk. Much like scientist Banner, students all over the country are coming to school with a backpack full of things we can't see. They are struggling with homelessness, sickness, abuse, poverty, parents in prison, death, and so much more. Unlike Dr. Banner, these students are real, and the problems they face are also real. They aren't fictitious characters in a movie, they are real people sitting in our classrooms trying to learn and overcome their trauma. You may be thinking, it's an invisible backpack they bring to school so how will I ever know what they struggle with? Consider this:

> When considering implementing trauma-informed practices in your school, you might find yourself asking: How do I know which students have experienced trauma, so I can teach those students in a trauma-informed way? While it's important to

identify students in need of extra support, we can use trauma-informed practices with every single student because they benefit them all. Think of a wheelchair-accessible ramp in a building: Not every single person needs it, but it significantly removes barriers for those who do, and signifies to everyone that the building is an accessible place. We can do the same thing for our students impacted by trauma when we remove barriers and use the trauma-informed strategies as a whole school. (Venet, 2017)

Trauma-informed instruction needs to be a top priority in all schools. Leaders need to be learning about trauma-informed instruction and working to design schools, learning, and culture around it. Building a trauma-informed school culture benefits all learners. You will notice a change in many ways, including four areas of culture: relationships, resources, interventions, and wisdom. Let's take a look at each of the four.

> Building a trauma-informed school culture benefits all learners.
>
> @DrBillZiegler @DrDaveRamage

A Culture of Relationships

Hero-building school leaders build positive and caring relationships with students. When they know we care, they are able to thrive and overcome insurmountable odds. When everyone in your building nurtures strong relationships with students and families, it transforms the school from a place we have to go to a place where students and staff want to be.

We believe Alfonz knew we cared about him and his growth as a person. We worked every day to make a personal connection with him and to let him know we were there for him. There's nothing more powerful in a school than adults who care for, support, nurture, and love students. When this takes place, students thrive. Schools should be safe harbors for students where they can connect with caring and loving adults and where they can dream about the future. By helping students dream and plan about the future, we provide them with hope of healing, hope of overcoming, hope of succeeding, and hope for the fulfillment of their dreams. School staff members have the ability to invest in a child's life in a way that makes them feel special, valued, and supported. When this happens, children flourish, and their dreams can come true.

Creating this kind of culture takes intentional action and considerable time. You probably feel like your list of must-do items is already far too extensive to accomplish, but adding ways to build a culture of relationships will not be wasted effort. Consider choosing a few students who would really benefit from a stronger connection to an adult who cares for them, and ask your teachers, aides, secretaries, custodians, counselors, and volunteers to do the same. Once each adult in the school has a student or two in mind we encourage you to try the "Ten, Two" (10/2) strategy. Simply make a commitment to have a two minute conversation with the student you identified for 10 days in a row. Make time at the start of the day, lunch, recess, study hall, or activity time to give that student two minutes of focused attention. Find out what he or she loves to do, how it's going at school and at home, what his or her dreams and aspirations are . . . in short, make an authentic connection. This simple, intentional investment will create a strong connection and help your whole school staff improve in their work to create a strong culture of relationships.

A Culture of Resources

I always wanted to visit the Batcave even though I knew it wasn't real. Batman had every kind of resource you could think of, and even those that never crossed your mind, in the Batcave. He had an amazing car, an even better motorcycle, the latest and greatest tech gadgets known to man, and hundreds of weapons that could stop any villain in their tracks. We can't transport students to school in the Batmobile, but why can't we equip our schools with the resources to help support students in their issues and struggles? We certainly have some resources to offer, and one of the most powerful is the people we can use to help students directly, and we can point them to the specialized, community resources they may need that fall beyond the scope of our school.

I am so grateful that our school district invested in hiring two social workers who support our students. They help students and families find resources for medical care, funding for eyeglasses, coats in the winter time, counseling supports, and so much more. These two people are precious gems in our district as they work to help families and students identify and locate the resources they need to function well. It's sad, but so many students today are coming to school hungry, lacking proper clothing, not having medical care, and without a home. Maslow's hierarchy of need's must be met before students can truly dig into learning and growth. Without the basic needs of food, water, warmth, shelter, healthcare, and love, students struggle to find their way and often are distracted in the learning process. That's why schools need to be helping kids beyond the classroom by connecting their families to community and local resources for support. More now than ever before, schools are going the extra mile in supporting students.

Bald Eagle Elementary School in Pennsylvania, with Principal Jim Orichosky, packs backpacks each week for their kids that are filled with nonperishable meals that they can eat over the weekend. We were shocked when the principal told us that every backpack is returned on Monday to get filled up for the end of the week. The school actually has a food bank that collects food for their kids and sends them home every weekend with meals, not just for the student but the entire family. Our Middle School in Pottsgrove has a similar backpack program for families that need food support. Some schools have a dental truck come to the school, others bring doctors in for checkups, and some even collect eyeglasses to give away to kids in need. One school in Kentucky built a mailbox-like structure outside of the school and filled it with food regularly. People can drive by the school and take out food whenever they are in need.

Our middle school and high school both have a one-to-one program called DiLE (Digital Learning Environment). Every middle school student receives an iPad device, and every high school student gets a MacBook laptop. Access to these devices helps bridge an equity divide where approximately 42 percent of our students are economically disadvantaged, and roughly 13 percent of our students do not have access to an Internet-connected device at home other than a cell phone. Most assignments can be completed offline and automatically synced when students return to school. However, for times when an assignment needs to be done online after school, our district purchased hotspots that students can sign out from the school library. This provides Internet access for students who lack that resource at home. How is your school working to support students with the resources they need for living and learning?

A CULTURE OF INTERVENTIONS

Schools that have systemwide interventions in place for all kids provide the supports needed for students facing trauma. Some educators would say these interventions are not fair, but an honest look at the interventions shows supporting students in need is required if we are really going to move these students forward. Adjusting deadlines, allowing for choice in learning, and providing time for tutoring and interventions in the day is critical. The old rule of learning was that if you needed tutoring, you stayed after school, and your parents picked you up. For many students, this is no longer a reality, that is why schools must design structured intervention time into the school day for tutoring, remediation, and academic monitoring.

Students also benefit when their school assigns a caring teacher to serve as a student's mentor or coach. This coach will check in on the children every day, connect with them about their life and schooling, and work with them to make sure they are learning and completing their work. This simple check-in process is powerful. It can happen with a counselor, social worker, or teacher, but we also had a custodian at our middle school who was masterful at connecting with some of our most fragile students. Bring your whole school community onboard to support your students.

> Too often we punish students when we should really be teaching them how to behave.
>
> @DrBillZiegler @DrDaveRamage

A culture of intervention is sometimes present in a school, or district, in a way that shows deep caring for students, yet uses inefficient practices to meet their academic, social, and emotional needs. Wayne Callender is an author and national RTI consultant who influenced the multi-tiered system of support (MTSS) we implemented in our K–5 schools. He urges schools to move from calling one meeting at a time to discuss ways to help an individual student who is struggling to instead beginning to design systems that take consistent data and connect students with interventions more quickly. This shift represents a change from the decades-old problem-solving approach to the more systemic approach of Standard Protocol (IRIS Center, 2006). Hero leaders find ways to build these systems of intervention so students benefit from all the resources the school can bring to the table. Supports need to extend beyond simply academic bolstering and gap closing to demonstrating our beliefs that every student needs a connection to the people at school. Designing systems that address academic struggles while fostering relationships in a safe space is the work to be done. As long as we have students who struggle, we will have a need for this vital work to continue. It must become more than a shared belief, it must become part of our culture.

A Culture of Wisdom

Schools need to take a new and wise approach to how we do things. For decades, we have been disciplining students the same way. It's time that we wise up and examine ways to provide a more restorative approach to discipline. This is especially important when we work with trauma-informed instruction, and it's vital to reimagine how we teach students about behavior. Think about it; if kids can't swim, we teach them how to swim. If kids can't read, we teach them how to read. If kids can't ride a bike, we teach them how to ride a bike. But what do we do when a kid can't behave properly? Too often we punish students when we should really be teaching them how to behave.

That's why positive behavior intervention and support systems are so important to teach behaviors and recognize students for doing the right things. We need to stop just suspending students out of school and look for ways to change behavior rather than simply punishing it. If we don't address the bigger issues with some thoughtfulness and wisdom, we will find a high rate of the same behaviors when students return to their school and classroom. You will find some powerful resources and ideas about positive behavior interventions and supports at www.pbis.org. Their resources apply to family and community settings in addition to their dedicated work for schools.

Every 22 seconds, a student drops out of school, and 25 percent of all high school freshmen fail to graduate on time or at all. Sadly, high school dropouts commit about 75 percent of the crimes in this nation (DoSomething.org, n.d.). Schools are thirsty for real innovation that rethinks how we do school. Our country is hungry for schools that are not preparing students for prison but for the workplace, college, and beyond. We must be wise enough to teach and expect positive behavior, design appropriate consequences for wrong behaviors, and build in ways to restore relationships so the downward cycle toward dropping out does not continue.

Wisdom is more than knowledge. Wisdom learns and then applies that learning to generate the best outcomes for the whole organization. Wisdom does not ignore the external pressures schools face from political rhetoric and wrong thinking about what constitutes great learning, but wisdom prevents us from joining the throngs who seek a reactionary, short-sighted, quick fix to a complicated, multilayered problem. The wise leader keeps a focus on relationships and quality learning that will serve our students in the years ahead. The kind of learning that remembers a large percentage of the jobs our current students will hold is yet to be invented. Preparing students for that kind of unknown future does not have to be impossible, it just requires us to consider the kinds of experiences we can design to equip our young learners with skills beyond memorization and rule following. We need to grow skills for lifelong success and produce students who can consider issues critically, work collaboratively, communicate clearly, and call on creativity for solutions. Too often we celebrate our work to produce creative problem solvers when all we're really doing is teaching students to follow a recipe to "solve" a hypothetical situation. We need to design experiences where students first learn to be creative problem finders. Once they identify the authentic problem, we also need to allow them to struggle for a powerful solution. The wise leader knows learning is hard work and does not settle for quick fixes or shortcuts to standardized testing boosts.

SEEING THE INVISIBLE

If a principal or teacher entered the Daily Planet newsroom in Metropolis, would they be able to scan the crowd and notice the amazing potential in one of the reporters working there? We all know Clark was trying to blend in with the crowd, but I can't help seeing the irony that it was his status quo, compliant mannerisms and behaviors that served his purpose of hiding in plain sight. Are schools guilty of promoting similar behavior? Do some students show up day after day, quietly fit in, and never become who they are meant to be? Whether you're a school leader, classroom teacher, or support staff member, are you missing what students and colleagues really bring along with them to school? Who's hiding in plain sight? Are we also dismissing every student who is not compliant as a person who doesn't care about learning, as someone who will never achieve success?

Many of us have been guilty of what John Holt (1995) identified in his seminal work, *How Children Fail*. We learned that if we are quiet, compliant, pleasant, raise our hands, and do our homework we can often manipulate the teacher to do most of our hard work for us. One of the problems in this scenario is many "successful students" fail to own their learning. They never develop the mindset, habits, or skills to remain lifelong learners after the school dismissal bell sounds. Adam Grant (2016) points to the surprising disconnect between the students winning the teachers' approval and the students who achieve the greatest career successes. The leaders who make their mark on society are often not the ones who reach the greatest level of teacher approval during their formative years.

So how do we see beyond the strong pull of schooling that has taught us—whether we realize it or not—that there's one way to do school? How do we learn that students aren't always what they seem to be? Our students can be wild, whispering, exuberant, exhausted, confident, or collapsed, but do we really know which ones are truly engaged in the learning we've planned? If they're thoughtful and reflective, are they considering the lesson or worried about the dinner meal they'll miss because the pantry at home is sparse? Is their homework missing because they don't care about grades, or were they responsible for feeding and supervising their young siblings while Mom worked her third-shift job?

As educator, author, and inspirational speaker Craig Boykin points out, "Circumstances trump curriculum" (2015).

We need learn to see the invisible kid. Similar to the way a hero can look through obstacles and disguises to see what truly lies beneath, we need to look beyond the exteriors that our students present. The shy student who never approaches you and does the work without the need for intervention. The one who only asks questions at home or with friends. The one who is never a problem in your classroom or school but never reaches the potential he or she could achieve with targeted support. Our leadership capital is often invested in our most struggling learners and our most precocious students, but we cannot abandon the students in the middle of achievement or we sacrifice their growth. We also fail to connect these students to a caring, emotionally safe community.

Super Hearing and Dangerous Thoughts

Whether heroes possess super hearing or attain it with technology-laden gear, the result is the same—they notice what others don't. In a world where more and more students struggle with adverse childhood experiences (ACES) and bring substantive mental health struggles to the classroom, we need to make sure our hearing is going well beyond what is easily heard. Sometimes the loudest messages, and cries for help, are unspoken. We need to listen closely enough to recognize them.

Paying attention to the warning signs our students "quietly speak" is more important than ever. Leaders cannot ignore the dangerous thoughts of self-harm, violence, and high-risk behavior that have become more and more common in our schools. The dangerous-thoughts students are those students that pose a serious threat to themselves and our schools if they are not identified, supported, reconnected, and cared for.

Later in this chapter, we provide a survey tool to use to identify if students are connected to a caring adult in your school. We passionately believe that all students need a caring adult who believes in them, knows them, and encourages them. We encourage you to use Figure 2.1, My Teacher Survey for Students, to identify students who you need to support and get connected in your school.

School leaders need to surround these students with the supports to build healthy relationships, connect them to appropriate professional help, and nurture trust with caring adults in the school community. We will also talk about the importance of leveraging family and community supports to come alongside these kids to help them overcome their challenges.

Leaders need to leverage community resources to support these students, whether it be counseling, therapy, or working with a social worker to attain the necessary supports to help these students find success. Our community has a great resource called the Montgomery County Mobile Crisis Unit. This unit supports students and families at their home or school. They provide supports with overcoming self-harm, suicidal thoughts, or other types of trauma. We have called them several times to support families, and families have found them tremendously resourceful and useful in helping them through trauma. Leaders need to know and understand the resources in their community and then know when to tap into them. Plus, leaders and their team can support families by helping them to connect to social services, learn about the resources available, and engage them to make connections with these varied resources. Schools need to be strategic places where students and families can go to find resources in their community. In addition, schools can use these resources strategically to help intervene for students with dangerous thoughts.

GAP KIDS

Sometimes heroes are faced with an almost impossible choice. We are sure you can picture the scenario where the bus full of children is teetering on the edge of a collapsing bridge while a mom with a small child in a stroller dangles from a ledge of a falling building. Where does the hero go first? In our movie plots, the hero miraculously saves them both, and we can, too (just not alone). What does this scenario have in common with our classrooms? We have some students who are in greater danger. Danger of disconnecting from education altogether because year after year the gaps they bring will grow and eventually lead them to throw up their hands and surrender to the struggle that learning has become.

These are the very students we need to grow further and faster—otherwise their learning gaps will persist. These are the students that are falling behind their peers and struggling in the classroom. School leaders have a moral responsibility to make sure that these students are given the tools to succeed, the supports to overcome their many obstacles, and the community to care for and love them in a powerful and meaningful way.

In the previous movie scenario, it's easy to see who is in the greatest peril. Seeing who we need to rescue most immediately in the classroom is not always so apparent. There is no substitute for building relationships with our students and knowing them well. Classroom teachers and interventionists may have the best chance to do this, but the school leader does not get a free pass. In fact, these are the very students the whole school community needs to rally around and encourage. With powerful data tools, authentic conversations, and caring relationships, we can pull these students back from the brink of their impending learning disaster. This is where the adults get to show their (collective) hero strength.

HIDDEN STRENGTH

Heroes do not focus on their weaknesses. Instead, they leverage their greatest strengths to make a difference and accomplish their mission. Too frequently we are guilty of ignoring our students' strengths to focus our attention, effort, and feedback on their weaknesses. We understand that allowing, or creating, gaps in skills and concepts needed in a

Figure 2.1   My Teacher Survey for Students

My Teacher . . .	No Way!	Not sure	Somewhat	Absolutely!
My teacher cares about me				
My teacher takes an interest in my life				
My teacher believes in me				
My teacher shows me that he or she cares				
My teacher greets me by name every day				
My teacher knows me as a person				
My teacher knows my strengths and passions				
My teacher knows my future dreams				
My teacher inspires me				
My teacher challenges me to grow as a student				
My teacher supports my learning				
My teacher engages me as a learner				
My teacher empowers me to learn				
My teacher is innovative				
My teacher uses technology to engage me as a learner				

progression of learning is not acceptable. Even when we are aware and concerned about gaps, we can make significant progress with the academic and social-emotional success of a student by affirming what he or she does best. The very gifts and strengths we ignore can sometimes become the vehicle to overcome the gap in understanding.

One practical way to use a student strength is to include that interest or strength in a more personalized approach to a skill the student is struggling with. I was fortunate to have an English Language Arts teacher in the middle school who worked with our most fragile readers. A few of the boys he worked with were especially reluctant readers. When that teacher used personal funds to expand his classroom library to include nonfiction texts about computer gaming and texts presented in graphic novel form, he won over his students, and they became some of the most voracious readers in their grade level. By getting to know his students, seeing their strengths and interests, and providing instruction that invited them to "get stronger," he won them over. Continued focus on text structures, main ideas, themes, and other core content was possible because it no longer felt disconnected and unattainable.

HERO SIGHTING

One experience many of us recall, from when we were high school students ourselves, is developing the art of becoming invisible. It is possible to appear slightly attentive, while avoiding direct eye gaze, avoiding excessive movement, shrinking slightly into the seat rather than sitting upright, or using bluffing tactics such as pretending to be reading or writing. (Hattie & Yates, 2014, p.47)

Reflect with your team. How will you work in the next week, month, and semester to build and deepen relationships in your school community?

Whether you teach kindergarten students, lead a building, or direct an entire district, we implore you to build relationships with those you lead and teach. Don't allow students, teachers, aides, secretaries, custodians, lunch staff, or anyone else in your care to "slip away." Engage and connect with every human being in your school or system so you can be heroes and build heroes.

HERO TRAINING

Use these activities to nurture your skills. Even better—gather with your team to embed these skills in your work and empower your students to become heroes that change their world.

1. What calms you? Take time to reflect on the events, environments, or experiences that help diminish your stress. Remember to keep these things going so you can remain calm when your students, or staff members, are escalating.
2. Ask your staff members to do what we just asked you in the first bullet. Dedicate part of a faculty meeting to give permission for your teachers and staff to spend time doing the things that will keep them calm, patient, and excited to keep working in stressful situations with kids who bring traumatic situations with them in their invisible backpacks.
3. Slow down, and take time to see. We don't need actual X-ray vision, we just need to slow down enough to pay attention to what's right in front of us. Take a notepad, notebook, or tablet (digital or analog), and sit in a gathering place in your school. Spend five or 10 minutes just observing and writing down some of the things you see. Get past the physical setting, and pay attention to what you see in the relationships that take place in front of you. Better yet, take note of what you don't see

happening that you hope will become a part of your school's culture and climate.

Have your students take the My Teacher Survey for Students (Figure 2.1). Gather the results so your teachers can reflect on the findings. Finally, bring your team together to discuss how you can help students get connected to a caring adult in your school.

3

TRUE TO LIFE LEADERSHIP AND LEARNING

"There are two kinds of people, those who do the work and those who take the credit. Try to be in the first group; there is less competition there."

—Indira Gandhi

Why is it less likely that you will be harmed by a lightning strike if it occurs in a car or other vehicle? I bet your answer was because the rubber tires protect the car and the occupants inside. Most of us grew up being taught that the rubber tires protected us from being struck by lightning because the rubber acted as insulation from the electric charge of lightning. That's a myth that has been passed down from generation to generation. [Bill] My son is an engineering student at Penn State University, and he shared with our family this week that what we believed our entire life was false. He explained how being inside the vehicle is like being inside a ball of charge. If the car is struck by lightning, the inside of the car is most likely safe even though touching the outside of the car would not be. According to Chrissy Warrilow, a reporter for the Weather Channel, "In actuality, lightning flows around the outside of a car, and the majority of the current flows from the car's metal cage into the ground below. In essence, a car acts like a mobile Faraday cage" (2016).

How is it that my wife and I (both of us college grads) believed this myth our entire lives? Statistically, chances are high that you believed it, too. It wasn't until our son introduced new information and facts about why people in cars don't typically get struck by lightning that I realized my thinking was wrong. He shared how it has more to do with the charge of the metal than it does the rubber tires acting as an insulator. I learned this myth from adults older than me, and they probably learned it from adults older than them. It's easy for us to pass on myths that we believe and even to defend them as being true. I have learned so much from students through the years, and this is one more example of how kids have so much to teach adults, and we have so much to learn from them. It's critical for adults to be open to learning new things, examining and challenging their own misconceptions, and working to move beyond the myths that hold us back.

> Kids have so much to teach adults, and we have so much to learn from them.
>
> @DrBillZiegler @DrDaveRamage

What myths are we carrying on in education that eat away at progress and growth? What mistruths are we perpetuating in our classrooms, schools, and communities? Which lies and myths about education and learning do we still believe even though they are no longer true? It's difficult for us to surrender and realize that our thinking may be wrong, but hey, we live in the world of Internet information now, and it's time that we double check our thinking and our sources.

It's sad that our kids are growing up in a world when so much misinformation is published on the Web. But what's even more disheartening is that our kids are being taught in ways that are no longer relevant. Common instructional methods are disconnected from research and data, and even well-meaning teachers are misguided. It's time that we face the myths we believe in regard to teaching our kids. Their future and our reputation depends on it. We need to help students see through the myths of our world and help them become truth detectors who sense when a lie, myth, or mistruth comes their way.

LIES WE TELL OURSELVES AND BELIEVE

[Bill] When I was in fifth grade, I got into a fight with my friend, Steve. He was coming off the soccer field in gym class, during what seemed to us like the World Cup, and I had a few choice words for his lack of performance. Well, we won't say who swung first, but we started fighting right in front of our peers and gym teacher. I'll never forget the gym teacher pulling us apart and realizing at that point that I was in big, I mean BIG, trouble. The teacher walked us to the principal's office, and I was scared to death at this point. I had never been in this kind of trouble before, and I knew my parents would be really disappointed in me. The principal knew my family well because my sister, who was four years older than me, was the top academic student in the school and received many accolades from the principal and her teachers. As I sat in front of the principal's desk explaining to him what I did and how sorry I was, I begged him to allow me to tell my parents before he called them. He agreed to allow me to go home and tell my parents, and I was to have my dad call him the next school day. Well, that fight was about to turn into a much bigger problem for me, as I didn't tell my parents. The next day the principal asked me if my dad was going to call. I shared that my grandfather was very sick, and my parents were tied up taking care of him as it was so sad for our family that he was sick. I promised my dad would call the next day. By the way, my grandfather was not sick at all, I just turned a fight into a huge lie that I had to keep covering up. I still can't believe to this day that I brought my innocent grandfather into this one. As with most lies, this one snowballed out of control.

The next day the principal asked me again, and I shared that my grandfather passed away, and our family was heartbroken. I still feel horrible to this day that I went that deep in lying. I went home, was convinced that I dodged this bullet, and moved on with life. Over the weekend, my mom and dad called me into the family room and wanted to talk to me. My dad asked, "How's school been going son?" I responded that school was great. Next he asked if I had any problems with anyone in school, and of course I said everything was great and that I had no problems. Then, it hit me like a bus, my dad asked, "How are you and Steve doing?" I sat there considering giving up and admitting my lies, but instead I held strong and continued fabricating story after story. It wasn't until my dad said, "I work with Steve's dad, and he told me everything," that I surrendered and admitted all my wrongdoings. My parents' trust in me was shattered and even worse was my reputation with my principal.

There are lies that we devise to overcome getting in trouble for a fight in the fifth grade, there's those little white lies that the world tells us are alright and they really aren't, and then there's the systemic mistruths that we tell ourselves as educators allowing us to believe these myths that need to be shattered for true learning and growth to take place.

We need school leaders who empower students to become heroes who know the truth and aren't afraid to face the myths and lies that they will hear throughout their lives. It's time that our students think differently in a world that is complex and challenging. We believe many of these myths are passed from one generation to another without ever examining if they are true or based on solid research. Helping students gain Web literacy skills is a key skill that is required for truth detection. We need to learn to rely on solid thinking skills and use the power of our computing devices as the secondary resource. Too often students, and leaders, take what they see at face value instead of engaging in higher-level, critical-thinking skills. Technology leaders like Alan November (2012) have stressed the need for schools to promote critical thinking skills related to Web literacy for years, and we need to heed the cry now more than ever!

In a world organized by likes, followers, retweets, and instant gratification, we need to remind ourselves that patience, critical thinking, and measured reasoning all seem countercultural but are exceptionally important habits to build.

HIGH RISK MEANS HIGH REWARDS

[Bill] My personality has always been attracted to high risks. I love the adventure and exhilarating experience of living life on the edge. I started teaching back in the '90s when the Internet came into our lives. Our school only had one Internet connection, and that was in the library. As a Government teacher, I wanted our students to have access to the Internet, so I researched how to install a modem into my computer and how to get Internet access. I bought a modem for my computer and cable to hook up my class computer to the library computer. One night, I went into school, installed my modem, and ran the cable down the hall (over the ceiling tiles) and into the library hooking it up to the library computer. The custodians thought I was crazy, and they were right, I was crazy. But, I was pumped that my class could get on the Internet. We worked to develop a pen pal in London, used the White House and Congress websites to learn about government, and were connecting with schools all over the world. On Back to School Night, I was thrilled to showcase our work to the parents. With my back to the screen as I was facing the parents and my computer, I typed in the Web address to the White House, after a few buzzing sounds of connecting to the Web, the website came up on the screen. I knew something was instantly wrong as I saw two mothers cover their mouths in awe, their eyes were huge, and some chuckles came from the room. As I turned to look at the screen, it felt like life was in slow motion at this point, as saw Hillary and Bill Clinton in ways that none of us should ever see them. I typed in the wrong Web address for the White House, and it took me to a pornographic website. I was so embarrassed, I just wanted to crawl into a cave and never come out. I deeply apologized and immediately ran down to the office to tell my principal. My principal was awesome! He chided me for doing this without his permission but supported me in overcoming this big mistake. My risk and drive to be the first in the school with Internet could have cost me my job. I learned that day that it's better to really think out what we are doing, to see if it aligns with our district's goals, vision, mission, and policies, and to reflect on my decisions.

Why do we get sucked into believing that true innovation requires us to take high risks that could cost us a great deal? We buy into the notion, "The bigger the risk, the bigger the reward." That only works in the lottery, and we don't know many people that have won the lottery. Instead, calculated risk is the best kind of risk that leads to innovation for school leaders. This risk requires school leaders to examine the costs, the connection to mission, and the value of student learning. We like to think of it as living safely dangerous; this is when we can take a risk, but we have measured the safety concerns over the risk. For example, we have always wanted to jump out of an airplane, and I'm sure sometime we will get our wish. However, we can assure you that we will not fly solo and take the leap out of the plane on our own. We plan on being tethered to a really big person who is highly skilled and has done that tons of times before jumping with us. You see, we will take the risk of jumping out of a plane, but we are not doing it alone! We don't trust our own skills, or lack thereof, to transport ourselves to the ground safely.

Far too often, high risks result in high loss and destroy trust and consensus you've built. Without thoughtful and strategic innovation, we fall into recklessly leading schools in a way that is not focused on progress, growth, and achievement.

Figure 3.1   FORWARD Check-in—Let's see how your team is doing on the FORWARD acronym.

Action	1—Needs improvement	2—Learning it	3—Got this, doing great	4—Total hero!	Notes
Focused					
One step at a time					
Reimagine					
We need to move together					
Achievement					
Reflection					
Dream together					

The same can be said with innovation in schools. Let's create risk that allows our students to grow and achieve without setting them back further. By doing this, we build capacity within the staff and support from our superiors. Let's take the time to risk safely, not dangerously—the future of our kids depends on it!

We would like you to consider this acronym before moving FORWARD with innovation and calculated risk-taking at your school:

> **F**—Focused: Is your innovation focused on your district's/school's missions, values, core beliefs, and goals?
> **O**—One step at a time: Way too often we rush by trying to skip past steps in order to innovate.
> **R**—Reimagine: Are you really doing something new or just repackaging something you've always done with a new name?
> **W**—We need to keep moving forward together!: True innovation moves people together.
> **A**—Achievement: Innovation needs to focus on progress, growth, and achievement.
> **R**—Reflection: Take time to reflect on the innovation and to see if it's meeting your intended goals.
> **D**—Dream Together: Begin to dream about how your school can be!

GROWTH CHALLENGE ON FORWARD RUBRIC

If you scored nine or less points, you may be stuck in old ways that are holding you back like an albatross around your neck. It's time to let go and to trust your team, seek ways to innovate within your setting, and take small steps to move forward. If you are in the 10 to 19 point range, you have some room to grow. We challenge you to self-reflect and collaborate with your team to reflect on where you need to move forward. Get connected to a professional learning network, attend a conference, journal your reflections, or visit an exemplary school in your community. Set aside time to plan some action steps, in writing, that help you and your team break through to the next level. For those in the 20 to 29 range, way to go! Keep moving forward and doing the great things you are doing. Take time to reflect and identify areas needing attention, push yourself to innovate, and take a risk that will stretch you and your team. We need to learn from you, so begin to give back to the profession by telling your story on social media. If you are in the 30 to 35 range, you are a total ROCKSTAR!!!! Way to go, you better be out telling your story on social media through pictures, video, blogging, and so on. School leaders need to be learning from you, so set up visits for educators to see the great things in your school, host a Facebook live session to showcase your work, and share your story on social media. We believe giving your best ideas away is a great way to keep generating innovation in your school and to strengthen leaders in your region.

Visit our website at www.chaselearning.org/herobuilding for resources on how to move FORWARD with innovation.

Failure Is an Option

We know that we all hear the words of the Apollo 13 team when we hear that phrase, "Failure is not an option." Well, those engineers didn't work in a school. You see, in a school, failure is an option that should be embraced (See Figure 3.2). We are not talking about the failing grade that requires one to repeat a course but the failure of a task, an attempt, or in trying something new. We need to foster and nurture a culture that embraces failure and the ability to fail. We say that purposely, the ability to fail, because that is a new concept for many leaders. Yes, having the ability to fail means that one's confidence, attitude, and mindset doesn't see failure as a setback but rather as an opportunity. As Thomas Edison shared, "I have not failed, I've just found 10,000 ways that won't work." As school leaders, we have a responsibility to model failure, trying again, and working through challenges, obstacles, and blockades that may get in our way. It's just as much

Figure 3.2   Failure Reflection

	Hide It	Own It	Share It
When I fail, I . . .			
When I struggle, I . . .			
When I make mistakes, I . . .			
When I mess up, I . . .			
When I fall short, I . . .			
When I flop, I . . .			
When I lose control, I . . .			

about resilience and perseverance as it is a mindset to move beyond the failure to success. We will provide school leaders with strategies to teach students how to fail forward and how to be resilient in all that they do.

Too often as leaders we try and hide our failures, struggles, and mishaps. Sometimes we own up to our mistakes, but rarely do we come out and share them. By sharing our mistakes, we build trust and foster an environment in which it's alright to fail. Without failure, it's challenging to move forward. When we share our failures and struggles, we are transparent and empower others to do the same. By teaching students this important principle, we empower them to overcome the challenges they will face, the failures they are bound to have, and to work through some of their darkest times of self-doubt. I'd like you to examine how you deal with failure and take a few moments to reflect and complete the Failure Reflection self-assessment.

HIDE YOUR MISTAKES AND WEAKNESSES

Many school leaders believe that they need to hide their mistakes and weaknesses from their faculty, staff, students, parents, and community. This fallacy and myth saps energy from school leaders as they strive to live a life of covering up or disguising their weaknesses. Plus, when we do this, we are teaching kids that they need to be ashamed of their mistakes and weaknesses. We need to know what our weaknesses are and when we make mistakes, they don't need to define us. By learning this life skill, we empower students to embrace who they are and not shy away from risk taking simply because it may lead to mistakes or failures. We help students become heroes by being confident in their weaknesses. When we say confident in their weaknesses, what we mean is that the students know their weaknesses and work to overcome them but not to the point that their focus on weaknesses overshadows their focus on strengths. The work of Carol Dweck (2016) shows us that we should be focusing on our strengths and leveraging resources around us to strengthen our weakness. Plus, kids need to learn that it's alright to make a mistake, that's how we learn and grow.

At a recent faculty and staff meeting, I (Bill) shared how my wife and I wanted to remodel our bathroom, so I took on the task with gusto and optimism. I have never done anything like this before, and a part of me was nervous in knowing that I am weak in the area of home improvements. However, I persevered and was determined to renovate our bathroom without the assistance of a professional. We replaced our flooring with vinyl plank flooring, and I laid the flooring while my wife was at work. When she got home, she asked why there were gaps between the planks. I told her I thought the planks would lock together at the end, I know this sounds totally crazy, but I believed it would all come together in the end. Wow, was I wrong. First, I decided not to read the directions. Next, I didn't even bother to watch a YouTube video, as I figured this wasn't rocket science, and I really expected I could do it.

After a 10-minute tutorial from my wife, I learned how to lock the planks together and make everything tight and waterproof. I needed to take out the toilet, so I watched some YouTube videos and knew I had this down. I finished the

Figure 3.3   Truth or Lie Self Reflection

Truth or Lie?	I don't believe this.	Yes, I believe it.	I believe, embrace, and live this.
1. I need to overcome my weaknesses and work to make them better.			
2. I grow when I develop my passions and strengths.			
3. I need to focus on my strengths and not my weaknesses.			
4. I am defined by my weaknesses.			
5. I need to surround myself with people that complement my strengths/weaknesses.			
6. I need to avoid mistakes at all cost.			
7. I should look to hire and be around people smarter than me.			
8. Sharing my mistakes, failures, and weaknesses is a weakness.			
9. I should use resources around me to strengthen my weaknesses.			
10. It's a sign of strength and courage to ask for help.			

floor, installed the sink, and put the toilet back on using a quick seal rather than the messy wax seal. Everything worked great, I overcame my fear of renovations, and I did it. I completed my bathroom without the help of a professional, well, at least for a day. My wife was working in the room below the bathroom when she felt something dripping on her head. She looked up, and you guessed it, the toilet was leaking through the floor. Ugh! I had to call a plumber to fix the toilet and a contractor to fix the ceiling in the room below. I learned three things as a leader from my bathroom renovation experience: (1.) Ask for help, don't be afraid to say you don't know something, (2.) Admit your weaknesses—don't hide behind the fact that, "I got this" and "I can do this," and (3.) Learn from your failures—we grow by learning from our mistakes and failures.

Take a look at Figure 3.3. We hope that you responded "Yes or I believe" to numbers 2, 3, 5, 7, 9, and 10, as these are the phrases that develop us as leaders. The other statements hold us back from flourishing as leaders, and that holds back our students, faculty, staff, and community.

Front Runners Win

In his book, *Originals*, Adam Grant (2016) shares a concept called the pioneer and settler principle. He discusses how pioneers rush into something new, they blaze the trail for others, and are often the first to break into the industry. We admire these kinds of leaders and businesses, and we see them as trendsetters. Grant notes that Americans believe strongly in a first-mover advantage. I'm sure you've heard the business axiom, we want to be leaders, not followers. However, Grant finds that the majority of early leaders find short-lived success. Instead, it's the settler who watches the pioneer break into the industry, learns from the pioneer's failures, understands the market from observation, and then builds a solid plan to introduce a revolutionary product—not just a new one. Grant (2016) contends,

Settlers are often branded as copycats, but this stereotype misses the mark. Instead of conforming to the existing demand, they bide their time until they're ready to introduce something new. They're often working on revolutionary products, services, or technologies within the category. (p. 104)

You don't need to be the trailblazing school leader that finds constant struggles in moving forward. It's alright to watch, evaluate, and then move thoughtfully into innovation. An articulate, thought out, and strategic focus strengthens school innovation as it builds internal capacity with staff, students, and parents. It's alright to learn and watch what other school leaders are doing and then to try it in your school. It makes you no less of an innovator.

As leaders, we can easily be pulled into the notion that innovation requires us to be the trailblazing cavalier leader who is doing something that is groundbreaking. Instead, we need to focus on three steps to develop high quality innovation: settling in, building innovation that is sustainable, and seeking to build consensus around our work. Otherwise, we are innovating alone, and the team around us sputters and loses trust with the leader. Let's take a closer look at these three steps to grow innovation in our school.

SETTLING

The first step is settling. Settling in occurs when we dig into something so deeply that we invest our time, money, dreams, and focus toward improving. This isn't meant to be the quick fix innovation that flames out but the innovation that observes, measures, and strategically moves forward to improve, strengthen, deepen, or advance progress for all in the school (Hargreaves & Fink, 2006). It's about observing the innovation of others and working to implement that into your own system in a way that personalizes it for your team and students. Creativity is needed for a solution that's right for your setting. Sir

Ken Robinson reminds us that creativity can be incremental. He also notes that creativity is more than imagination, it's putting your imagination to work (Robinson & Aronica, 2015).

SUSTAINABILITY

Next is sustainability. As leaders it is so easy to fall into the mode of trying the latest gadget or jumping on the most current movement just because it sounds like the solution to all of your problems or because it looks amazing. This will show my age, but I remember as a young leader thinking whatever was on the cover of a certain educational journal to be the latest and greatest idea that I had to implement. Now, I examine if the innovation is a good fit for our school and culture by vetting it through a team and seeing if it aligns to our goals, vision, and mission. I believe social media has created exponential opportunities for leaders to constantly be seeing cool innovative things that they want to try in their school without working to align them to their school's mission and goals. When this takes place, the innovation dies out when funding dries up, the leader is distracted by the next innovation, or the leader moves out of that position. True innovation that works is innovation that is sustainable regardless if that leader moves to a different position.

CONSENSUS

Finally, we consider consensus. Far too often, leaders move innovation forward as the lone wolf rather than as a team. The heroes in the Avengers and Justice League are much stronger together because they complement one another's strengths and weaknesses. When these heroes join together to overcome a common nemesis, they are stronger. I love to watch the banter back and forth between Iron Man and Captain America as they both brag about their strengths and what makes them great, but they put their own egos aside to take on the threat to

Figure 3.4   Front Runner Self-reflection

	Always—1 Pt	Usually—2 Pts	Sometimes—3 Pts	Never—4 Pts
I want to be the first to . . .				
I jump at the first chance to . . .				
I need to be the first to have or share an idea				
I need to get and use the latest gadget or technology				
I innovate just to innovate				
I'm always on the lookout for the next new idea				
I believe front runners always win				
I want to be the first to share the latest scoop or news on . . .				
Something new scares me				
I do something no one has ever done before . . .				
Total Points				

society. When we can build consensus around innovation, we become heroes to our faculty and staff members because they are empowered to reach new heights they never thought possible. The same takes place when we seek consensus with students; we empower them to lead in a way that provides real and systemic change for our world. Our world needs leaders who can put aside their own greedy egos and desires to be the first to innovate and move toward building consensus and collaboration around innovation.

Take at look at Figure 3.4 and fill out the table there. Total Score Reflection: Tally up your score, and see where you align on the Front Runners-self Reflection.

10 to 18 points: You love to rush in without weighing the costs, looking at different perspectives, and taking high risks. You believe that high risks equals high rewards.

19 to 31 points: You may rush or hold back, consider the consequences, and begin to examine different perspectives. You may believe that high risk equals high rewards.

32 to 40: You thoughtfully wait before rushing in, consider ways to improve the ideas of others, and measure to avoid high risk. You believe calculated risk equals high reward.

INNOVATION IS FOR CRAZY PEOPLE

Well this may be partially true as we know some crazy school leaders who innovate. However, innovation is for everyone, you don't need to be crazy to be an innovative leader! School leaders can no longer afford to ignore innovation in learning, schools, and in creating a positive school culture. You see, innovation is now a job requirement for school leaders to design and lead schools in a way that truly prepares students for the future. If you think you do not have the ability to be an innovator, you are wrong. Because we believe anyone who has the passion, desire, and fortitude to be a school leader has ability to be an innovator. We see innovation as looking at and doing things in a new way that is creative and focused on improvement. It's seeing things differently, challenging the status quo, and working to improve the world. You may be innovative in your thinking around how to increase attendance in your school, how to design a new traffic flow at lunchtime, or how to engage students in a new way. There is a huge misconception that innovation requires the use of technology. Don't get us wrong, innovation will often align with advancements in technology, but it's not required to be considered innovation. You may be innovative in how you lead social-emotional learning in your school or how you work to build a positive culture and community. Don't hide your innovative ideas, share them with other school leaders. We grow by learning from other innovators.

How can educational leaders design learning in a way that students want to run to school rather than away from it? This challenge can be daunting, but it's one that requires our full focus as we strive to design schools where students see a practical and relevant connection, creativity being nurtured, and real-world problems being solved. This requires school leaders to think differently and to innovate.

The term *digital leader* should be synonymous with an innovative leader focused on learning. No longer can we simply lead in a digital environment; instead, we need to be innovative thinkers and leaders who are committed to student learning and growing equitable and culturally responsive schools. Below are four mindsets to help us LEAP into innovation:

- **Learning mindset**—School leaders need to be voracious learners who are constantly reading, networking, and growing as leaders and learners. Every leader needs to develop their personal learning network to stretch and grow. Digital tools can really expand your learning reach and options.
- **Empowering mindset**—For true growth and sustainability to take place with innovation in learning, school leaders need to empower others to lead. Invest in your teachers and students, challenge them, and inspire them to try new things and to innovate in their teaching practices and learning habits.

- **Advanced mindset**—School leaders need to have a mindset that hungers to advance the learning and growth of students and their staff. We need to move beyond the status quo and into a culture of growth and progress for all. It's critical that school leaders focus on nurturing, developing, and advancing their staff as much as students. A true learning culture focuses on both!
- **Practical mindset**—Innovation that inspires is innovation that solves real-world problems and makes practical connections to life. We can't innovate to entertain; instead, we must innovate to make a difference in our world. This reminds me of the student who desired to make a prosthetic hand for one of his classmates, so he and his teacher accepted the Prosthetic Kids Hand Challenge and did just that. Learn more at http://www.handchallenge.com.

LEADERS MUST BE THE LOUDEST VOICE

So many school leaders believe that their voice needs to be the loudest in the school. They need to be at the forefront of every-thing that goes on, and they need to be the loud, charismatic, and dominating leader. Ironically, the loudest voice could also be the quiet, focused leader who creates an environment of trust and keeps an amazing mission in front of their followers. Leadership isn't as much about a particular personality type as it is the focus to build consensus and collaboration around what's best for kids. The quiet, unassuming leader can be just as successful as the charismatic leader.

We believe the loudest voice is the consensus voice, where everyone comes together, listens to each other, and works to live out the school's mission and purpose. The super school works to promote student voice and choice in all aspects of the school. Reflect on how your school empowers student voice by completing Figure 3.5.

Figure 3.5   Loudest Voice in the School

Who is the loudest voice in your school?	On a Scale of 1 to 10, rank the voices in your school, with 1 being the softest voice and 10 being the loudest voice in the school.	Notes—explain why you gave the number you did.
Principal Team		
Faculty		
Staff		
Students		
Parents		
District Leaders		
Board of Directors		
Other		

There are effective leaders who are quiet, reflective, intro-verted, focused, intellectual, and dedicated to a systematic approach to leadership. This can be just as powerful as the high energy, engaging, personable, and extroverted leader. I recently read a story where a keynote speaker shared how the extroverts of the world love to have icebreakers where they need to talk to people or try something new and fun. The key-note speaker shared that his icebreaker would require every-one, extroverts included, to go in a room by themselves and read a book. Why do we generally think of leadership from an extrovert's perspective? It's important that we balance the extroverted and introverted in our leadership to connect to a diverse audience.

The loudest voice in the school cannot be the leader, it must be the team. We are all familiar with the phrases, "There is no I in team," or "We is better than I." But do we really prac-tice that in our leadership? Whose voice do our followers hear the most?

HERO SIGHTING

"Exposure to successful performances may not, within itself, constitute a viable modelling stimulus for learning. If it did, we could become musicians through attending a concert, or play excellent tennis after watching Wimbledon finals" (Hattie & Yates, 2014, p. 73).

Reflect with your team. What steps can you take to raise the quality of feedback that you give to students about their academic performance? Their social/emotional learning? To your staff as they work to create hero-building experiences for students?

We suspect your origin story includes a desire to change the world for your students. The findings by Hattie and his team are reminders to make sure you increase success in your hero-building quest by designing learning that includes clear instructions, encouragement, appropriate scaffolding, and an intentional practice in a setting where immediate, focused feedback is offered at a high level. Design your next lesson, or conduct your next classroom walkthrough, with this in mind.

HERO TRAINING

Use these activities to nurture your skills. Even better—gather with your team to embed these skills in your work and empower your students to become heroes that change their world.

1. Hero SIM: Visit our website at www.chaselearning.org/herobuilding, and complete the *3.0 SIM on Detecting Truths as a Leader.*
2. Work with your leadership team, and complete Figures 3.1 through 3.5 together.
3. Have your students and teachers work on Figure 3.5, Loudest Voice in the School, and collaborate as a team regarding what you learned from the responses.
4. Go to our website, and take the LEAP Leadership Survey to see how you can grow as an innovative leader.

4

UNLEASH THE VOICE AND CHOICE OF STUDENTS

"It took me quite a long time to develop a voice, and now that I have it, I am not going to be silent."

—Madeleine Albright

I t's a lot of fun to watch a great hero movie. Even better is watching hero students as they challenge the problems of our world and push toward a creative solution. When we think of hero students, we think of Sarah Pennington. Sarah is a graduate of Pottsgrove High School who has become a global game changer in the area of mental health for students. Sarah grew up with trichotillomania, a hair pulling disorder, that caused her anxiety and depression through her adolescent and young adult years. This disorder has caused her to engage in self-harming behaviors and even to consider ending her own life. Sarah has refused to allow this disorder to define her as a person. Instead, she has worked to be a survivor and overcomer who uses her disorder to inspire others. During her junior year, Sarah met with me to see if she could share her struggles with students in an assembly that she would lead on the topic of mental health. At this time, she was recognized nationally for her efforts in bringing awareness to mental health for students. We connected with Sarah's mom about the request, and we began to strategize what this would look like. We must admit, we were afraid to host a student-led assembly and especially an assembly on mental health led by a student. This terrified us as a school leadership team that is responsible for the message our students would receive. After much thought and reflection, we decided to partner with Sarah and her family to allow her to lead an assembly for our entire student body on the topic of mental health. Looking back, that was one of the best decisions we ever made as a school leadership team. That day, when we put our fears aside, we opened the door, no, we opened the floodgates, to increase student voice in our school. Ever since then, our school has been changed by the inspiring story and voice of one student, Sarah Pennington.

After months of planning and organizing the specific elements of the presentation, it was time for the assembly. During the assembly, Sarah stood before her peers, shared her personal battle with mental health struggles, showed pictures of her during her darkest times, and shared how she is working every day to be a survivor and overcomer. She provided warning signs for students, ways to get help, and inspiration to come forward if they were struggling with mental health challenges in their own life. Her story inspired students to come forward and ask for help for depression, anxiety, and other challenges with mental health. Today, Sarah continues to champion the cause of mental health with teens. She was recently recognized for her tireless work by being featured on the *Today Show With Megyn Kelly*, and she continues to inspire others to be overcomers and survivors.

Sarah's courage is an inspiration to us, and it also challenged us to consider what it means to promote student voice in school. Unleashing student voice is not easy, but it is worth it. As a matter of fact, it's required in today's age to prepare students to be productive and contributing members of society who are changing our world for good. Student learning can no longer be characterized as sitting quietly listening to the teacher all day. It's time to empower our students to become the heroes they were created to be. To unleash this superpower, school leaders must provide strategic and practical ways to nurture, foster, and grow student voice and choice in schools. We must promote a culture of student voice and choice in every aspect of school life. For students to have a voice and choice our school and world, school leaders must be strategic in their approach to develop this with faculty, model it themselves in the school, and provide a myriad of opportunities for student voice and choice to flourish.

> Unleashing student voice is not easy, but it is worth it.
>
> @DrBilZiegler @DrDaveRamage

IS YOUR HEARING GOOD?

[Bill] Over the past five to seven years, I have noticed a major decrease in my hearing. When I'm in a crowd, I can barely hear the voices of women or children. I struggle with high-pitched voices and noises. About a year ago, our family was driving our Honda Pilot on a road trip to Washington, DC. My wife and kids kept saying that the brakes needed to be replaced, and I wondered how they knew, as I didn't sense anything different, and the car seemed to handle well. As we pulled into a drive through window to pick up our food, my kids said, "Oh that sound drives me nuts." I had no clue what they were talking about because I didn't hear anything. They were hearing the wheels squeal, and all I heard was the man asking if my order was correct. I fought the fact that I had a problem for years. As far as I was concerned, my hearing was good, sufficient, and not in need of improvement.

One Saturday morning, my wife came in the house and yelled upstairs, "Jed ran away." Jed is our golden retriever. I heard my wife said, "Gabe ran away." Gabe is our kindergarten student next door neighbor. I couldn't believe Gabe ran away as he seemed to really love his family. I responded, "Why did Gabe run away?" My wife reiterated that Jed ran away. We went back and forth before I realized what she was trying to say, and I came downstairs to help her find our dog. For years, my wife, kids, family, friends, and coworkers told me that I had a hearing problem, but I thought I was normal. Having my TV volume on level 60 was normal, turning my car radio all the way up was normal, and having my phone volume on high was normal. I even thought the volume levels in my phone were broken because I couldn't hear my phone as well as I thought I should be able to.

Realizing I had a problem, I asked our school nurse to give me the normal hearing test that she gives our students. The nurse gave me a headset, sat behind me, and told me to raise my hand when I heard a beep. Well, I sat there for a while wondering when she would start the test, only to find out that she did start, and I wasn't hearing the beeps. The test ended, and my nurse told me to see a hearing doctor because I failed the test. Three additional failed hearing tests later, I still fought the fact that I had hearing loss. The doctors concluded that I have moderate to severe hearing loss, and it will never get better.

I finally had enough and decided to explore hearing aids. I thought, "I'm way too young to get hearing aids, they are for older people, not me." But I did it, I got hearing aids. When I walked out of the hearing aid office, I heard the birds for the first time in a long time, I heard the snow crackle below my feet like I haven't heard in years, and I realized that I was missing so much. I'll never forget when I came home and was standing in the kitchen with my wife and kids. I said, shhh, shhh, do you hear that? They responded, yes, dad, that's the refrigerator, and it's been that way for years. I heard noises I never heard before.

Do you think your hearing of student voice in your school is good when you really need hearing aids to detect what they are saying? Reflect on your practice using Figure 4.1. Are you deaf to the voice of students? I couldn't hear high frequencies even though I had no issue with the

Figure 4.1   Self-Reflection on Listening to Student Voice (Place an x in the box that best describes you or your leadership team.)

The District/School Leader . . .	Low Frequency— little or not at all	Medium Frequency— sometimes, but it's inconsistent	High Frequency— regular, often, a systemic approach
Regularly talks with students about how to improve the school			
Asks students what is going well and what they love about the school			
Eats lunch with students to connect with them and hear from them			
Asks students what they are learning			
Asks students how they can strengthen and deepen their learning			
Regularly talks with an advisory group of students about issues going on in the school			
Talks to students about what is important to them			
Works to connect and talk to all groups of students in the school			
Has a structured system in place to hear and listen from students			
Reads, reviews, and observes student work			
Listens as students explain their work, projects, and designs			

low frequencies. Are you hearing one group of students but not all? Ask your students, they will tell you if they feel heard and valued in your school. Unleashing the voice of students is something that we must do intentionally, with a focused strategy, and in a way that is sustainable over time. It needs to become part of your regular practice and school culture. The inclusion of student voice in schools is more important now than ever before.

> Student voice programs demonstrate a commitment to the facilitation of student agency and to the creation of policies, practices, and programs that revolve around the students' interests and needs. In this era of standardization and the Common Core, the practice of elevating student voice might seem countercultural, but given the importance of agency, autonomy, and self-regulation in student learning, it is really rather commonsensical. (Toshalis & Nakkula, 2012)

The other thing I began to realize is that there is a major difference between hearing and listening. When we listen to student voice and choice, great things happen, and students are empowered to be leaders who are ready and equipped to change our world for good.

Benefits of Listening to Student Voice and Choice

When we unleash student voice in our schools, students are empowered, and their learning is strengthened. Students take pride in their work, sense value in the daily work, and become an integral member of the leadership of the school. It's more than this. When student voice and choice is unleashed in the school, students know that the decisions made in the school are made in the best interest of them as students. They play a key part in moving change forward, building a positive school culture, and in providing real and sustainable positive change for the learning of all students. When students can say,

"My principal used my ideas to change the school!" the entire school culture becomes stronger.

School Reform Through Student Voice

Some leaders believe if they give a survey once in a while during the school year they have checked off the box of listening to students. Unleashing student voice and choice is so much more than this. It's empowering students with the ability to make decisions that directly affect their schooling, culture, and learning. Students need to be at the table when it comes to school reform. For far too long, adults in the school have chosen to ignore the voice of students as they work to improve the school. We believe that adults in the school can learn a great deal from all students—kindergarteners to high school seniors. Many adults discount the voice of younger kids because they are small and young. This needs to stop. We need to have all students, we emphasize *all*, at the table. When we say all, we mean students from every part of your school, from your life skills class to your gifted classes. Make sure all demographics, diverse groups, and levels of students are included in the discussion.

George Couros (2016) nails it in his *The Principal of Change* blog when he says, "They (students) have to be part of the solution." When students are part of the reform, they own it, embrace it, and lead it. Plus, our school reform process is strengthened. Many of us are afraid to listen to student voice because we may not like what they have to say. It can be difficult hearing some of the things they say about school reform, but it's time to peel away the Band-Aid and get your school equipped to listen to student voice. Do your policies, procedures, and regular practice embed regular and systemic avenues to have students involved in the decision-making process? Consider ways that you can redesign your thinking, your policies, and your routine procedures to further deepen the voice of students.

It's time we empower students to make their voice and choice heard in our school, community, and world; the future of our civilization depends on it! When we unleash student voice in the school, we not only improve the school, but more importantly, we empower students to advocate, learn, influence, and lead. By doing this, we are preparing them for the rapidly emerging challenges of our world. Be sure to include a diverse range of students in your focus groups. Students struggling in poverty are helped tremendously by being asked for their input, especially when their voice results in action by authority figures like a school principal (Jensen, 2016). By listening to students and sharing power for decision making with students you are helping them engage in their own successes in the classroom, in your school's goals, and in their partnership to improve the culture of your school community (Quaglia & Corso, 2014).

Our district (Pottsgrove School District) values student voice so much that we have placed two students to serve on the Board of School Directors as student board representatives. These students sit at the table during our Board of Directors meetings, they give a report on student voice and activities in the district, and they serve as representatives for our students to the school board. Our student board reps visit all five schools in our district to hear from students and learn what's going on at the different levels. Our school board members will reach out and ask the student board reps for their opinions and thoughts on various items during the board meetings.

Our student representatives are much more than figureheads. Reflect on how your student voices effect change with Figure 4.2. The district values their input at board meetings, and the high school turns their input into action. One of the students shared this reflection at a recent board meeting:

> One of the big challenges for us is implementing the ideas we have, and the ideas we get from the students, into the school. Whether it's us communicating it correctly with you guys (school board) or to Dr. Ziegler—or it's us not understanding what the students are saying.

Figure 4.2   School Reform Reflection

	Never	Sometimes	Always
Students are represented on our School Board of Directors.			
Students are represented on the school leadership team.			
Students have a voice in the reform and redesign of the school.			
Students meet with the school administrative team regularly to see how the school can be improved.			
Policies, procedures, and practices are infused with student voice.			
We do more than ask for student feedback. Student ideas are used to originate policies and procedures.			
Students regularly contribute to the positive change in the school.			

These are students whose voices make a difference!

In addition, our student board reps lead reform in our school. Last year, they were instrumental in the redesign and revision of our dress code. When we elected to update our dress code to meet the needs of our current trends, we included parents, students, and teachers in our discussion groups. Our student board reps also worked with other students in our school to voice their opinions in support of the victims and survivors of the mass shooting at Parkland High School. When students are active participants of school reform, the school is redesigned in an entirely new way. If students aren't a key partner in leading the reform in your school, that reform will not be sustainable or build consensus.

SOCIAL MEDIA AND STUDENT VOICE

Social media is definitely one area in which we hear adults saying that students are way too engaged. "They are always on their phone, they don't know how to have a real conversation, they'd rather talk to someone over social media than have a real conversation, they are losing connections." These are all statements we have heard adults say about kids and how they use social media. Well, these statements may be true for some students but certainly not all. We know a countless number of teens who are leveraging social media to deepen relationships, to foster new relationships, and to nurture existing friendships. We must jump into the world of social media with students if we hope to remain relevant to them.

Twitter Student Takeover—just the sound of those words is enough to send chills through the spine of many school leaders. Who would ever allow students to take over the school's Twitter account? We would. A few years ago, we gave control of our school's Twitter account to a student for the day. We wanted our community to view our school from a student's perspective. A Twitter Student Takeover is a powerful way for your community to see a sneak peek into the school from a student's perspective. Here are some clear steps we took to make sure that the Twitter Student Takeover was successful. In a 2014 newspaper article on our Twitter Student Takeover, I shared, "We didn't want someone who was new to Twitter. We also picked Shelby because she's relational, she knows how to connect with students and that was important to tell the story" (Brandt, 2014). Visit our website at www.chaselearning.org/herobuilding to read the article in its entirety.

- **Student Selection**—We selected a student who we knew was familiar with social media and its power to make connections. We intentionally selected a student who was already highly relational and one who reached a diverse group of students.
- **Parent Meeting**—We connected with the student's parents to set guidelines and to build a partnership in this adventure. This parent meeting is important to build trust with the student and to set clear guidelines and expectations.
- **Student Contract**—We reviewed the Student Takeover Contract with the student, and we explained our expectations, limitations, and requirements. The student contract set forth expectations, but it also provided some examples for the student to showcase throughout the day.
- **Monitor**—We monitored the account all day and had the ability to make changes, delete a post, or make suggestions at any time throughout the day.
- **Secure**—We kept the password and provided the student with a school issued iPad to enter her tweets. We reset the password for the day and changed it back after the student was finished using the Twitter account.

Twitter Student Takeover is just one example of how to infuse student voice into social media. Using video tools like Facebook Live and YoutubeLive are great ways to have students share what they are learning and great things that are going on in your school and classroom, and to connect with their community in new and engaging ways. Instagram, Facebook, and Snapchat provide features to shoot short one-minute or less videos to showcase and tell the stories of students. Leverage these platforms and new ones as they develop to tell the stories and learnings of students. Be constantly thinking about how you can turn over the microphone to students.

If you'd like to try this in your school, it's probably best to host an Instagram Takeover day and allow the student to post pics about their school day. This will gather huge support from fellow students and be a catalyst in building and promoting student voice in your school. The Common Sense Media (2018) study, *Social Media, Social Life*, shows that Instagram is the social media platform of choice for our school-aged kids.

Our librarian, Mrs. Dani Small, has students present one-minute videos on Instagram of books that they read to provide a description of the book. This works twofold, it provides an opportunity for students to showcase what they are reading, and it gives students a quick summary of potential books that they could be reading from the library. Mrs. Small often uses Instagram to showcase student work and voice, previews for students on great reads in the library, and shares how students are making and creating in the library.

Letting Students Lead

When students lead faculty meetings and professional learning for staff, it models to the faculty and staff the value you place on student leadership and student voice. It also encourages teachers to give over more power and control to students in their classes on a regular basis. Student-led professional learning for faculty and staff flips the table of teacher and learner. The faculty and staff become the students, and the students are the teachers. This powerful interaction is integral in developing a culture of student voice in your school. At our school, we have had students assist in leading professional learning around technology, our LGBTQ group came and presented on what it's like to be a LGBTQ student at our school, and Sarah Pennington shared with our staff about her work in the area of mental health.

Student-led parent/teacher conferences are another way to take student voice to a new level. Teach students how to lead their own conferences when it's time for parent teacher conferences. We shared this idea in our earlier book, *Future Focused Leaders* The ways of parent teacher conferences where the teacher sits behind the desk, reviews the student's grades, and simply asks the parents if they have any questions need to be updated. Students need to be an integral part of reflecting and reporting on their learning strengths, learning struggles, and progress in learning during parent teacher conferences (Ziegler & Ramage, 2017).

John Osgood, and his teaching staff at C. L. Jones Middle School in Minden, NE, host student-led conferences every school year. In the fall, the traditional parent teacher conference is held, but in the spring, students lead the conferences. Students have a series of instruments that are put together for them to work on. These include a grade sheet and examples of their work. They choose two items, and the teacher picks two items to reflect the quality of student work. The students do a self-assessment on how they feel about the class, their abilities in the class, and how they are doing in the class, and the teachers add to the assessment on how the student is doing on the same page so the parent can see both reflections. They also work on social structures where the students build a coat of arms that identifies them as a student, who their friends are, their interests, and things they like to do in school and out of school, and the students develop a script on what to do during the parent conference. Since they are a one-to-one school with iPads, the students are beginning to move all of this work into a digital portfolio, and the goal is to have students present their portfolio using the iPad with parents. The students also set academic goals for the year, and they measure the goals to check on their progress. The conference sessions are set up in the classrooms, so there are typically about four to five conferences going on in the same room. There is a gap between the conferences to meet the teacher and to get more information from the teacher, and the teacher meets up with the student and the parents to triangulate what the student shared during the student-led conference. Parent turnout for student-led conferences is 95–100 percent, but it was only 65–70 percent before student-led conferences. School leader John Osgood shares, "We have a lot more parents coming into the building, and students are accountable for their own learning."

The Board of School Directors is another great place to include student voice. One thing our district does is to dedicate time before school board meetings for students to teach our Board of Directors and central office staff something they are learning about. One of our elementary schools had students teach board members about STEM education and what they were doing in class. They also showcased how they were using technology to learn and engage with the world. When these partnerships develop over learning, a district's focus is driven toward involving students in all aspects of the school and district. Seeing the members of our school board and the superintendent engaging in a STEM task with our second graders is a powerful image that speaks loudly about the authentic culture of shared learning we are caring for and creating.

We also have two student representatives seated at the board table for our monthly meetings. There is a standing agenda item for student board representative reports. We intentionally appoint a member of the junior class and a member of the senior class of the high school to serve. This allows some instant mentoring from student to student and encourages new student members by placing them in a situation where they are not a one-and-only. Since this has been a part of our practice for several years, the board members themselves will often turn to student representatives for their ideas or input when discussion items arise. Never underestimate the poise, clarity, and insight that our students can lend to pressing matters. We don't just talk about honoring student voice, we allow student voice to authentically contribute to the decision-making process at the highest levels of our organization.

GAUGE YOUR STUDENT VOICE LEVEL

This self-reflection survey will help you see areas in which you're doing well and places you can focus on to increase the level of student voice in your school. Look at the indicators, and decide where your school fits within the four categories: low whisper, library chat, presenter voice, or shout. A low whisper is only heard by the person who is next to you and leaning in. A library chat is still a quiet conversation, but someone nearby may be able to hear it. A presenter voice is heard by all parties in the room, and it has an audience who wants to hear what's being said. A shout gets your attention and carries a long way. You hear a shout whether you are expecting it or not. We don't mean to imply the loudest voice should get the attention, this is about the response of your culture to listen to, and value, students' ideas and leadership. If you struggle to hear students' voices you may need them to speak more loudly, but you may also need a hearing aid.

Engaging and promoting student voice is so much more than just listening to students or giving them an avenue to express themselves. Use Figure 4.3 to check for student voice levels. It's featuring and making their work and learning the center point of the school. We have the best art teachers at our school; they love to post student work and celebrate all of the work of students, not just the best art students. Awhile back, our art teachers asked for bulletin boards to line our hallways from floor to ceiling. Since we installed the bulletin boards, our art teachers keep these board filled with student art, and they showcase the work of their students. When you walk into our school, you can clearly see that we value student

Figure 4.3   Gauge Your Student Voice Level Tool

Gauge Your Student Voice Level				
Indicator	Low Whisper	Library Chat	Presenter Voice	Shout It Out!!
Daily Schedule	The school chooses the schedule for the student.	The school allows the students to select their electives, but main courses are already decided.	The students have selection over their courses with limited flexibility and movement.	Students select their courses and have the freedom to make adjustments by dropping/adding.
Technology	Technology has no place in the classroom. If you bring it to school, it has to be locked in your locker.	You realize students use technology everyday outside of school but only allow phones during lunch.	You heard the students asking to learn in new ways and honor their preference with BYOD or by providing devices.	Devices are provided by the school, and an environment that extends the classroom beyond the existing walls allows students to learn 24/7 and share their solutions with the world.
Decision Making	Principals decide.	Teachers have a voice for students.	Students are at the table.	Student ideas are sought after, heard, and used.

Discipline Code	Code in place but has no student input.	Code is written by adults and communicated to students and families.	Students help write the discipline code, and their ideas are used in the final product.	Peer mediation is a big part of your discipline process.
Service Project	Students talk about community groups they'd like to support, but nothing ever happens.	One fundraiser was dedicated to a local group where some students volunteer.	Fundraising goes to projects identified by students and chosen by students.	Students identify organizations to support and organize events to raise funds for the organizations.
Dress Code	Students must wear a school-issued uniform.	Code written by adults and communicated to students and families.	Students help write the dress code policy, and their ideas are used in final product.	Student input throughout policy, and they communicate expectations to peers.
Your Area of Focus			
Your Area of Focus			

artwork, and in turn, we value student voice and expression through art.

It doesn't stop with art; valuing student expression through music, theatre, sports, writing, literature, and every other part of our high school is demonstrating a culture where students are authentically heard. Thanks to the leadership of Mrs. Caldwell, a Spanish teacher and veteran member of the Pottsgrove High School staff, our school publishes a literary magazine each year that highlights student writing, poetry, art, and expressions. This publication is very special and cherished by all who read it. Last year, we had a senior who loved to express himself through poetry. At different events during the school year, we asked him to write a poem and read it to the student body. Promoting student voice is much louder when we include all aspects of student expression into the school and community. Here are some powerful ways to integrate student expression into your school:

What do paper towels, hot sauce, a salad bar, and excused tardiness to school all have in common? You are probably thinking they have nothing in common. But, in our school, these are all items that our students have requested during our Falcon Feedback Friday session. Falcon Feedback Friday is Period 2 during the school day when I meet with four students from each grade, our student government president, and our student representatives to the school board. Students are selected randomly, and a new set of students is selected each week. During this time, we ask the students four questions:

Figure 4.4   Falcon Feedback Friday Questions

	Falcon Feedback Friday
1.	What does our school do great?
2.	How can our school improve?
3.	What do you dream our school can be?
4.	What can you personally do to make our school a better place?

Figure 4.5   Celebrating Student Voice Through Expression

	Expected	Engaging	Extraordinary
Design	Student artwork is posted throughout the school.	Student artwork is posted throughout the community.	Students design your school logo or gear to wear for students and staff.
Work	Student work is posted throughout the school.	Student work is posted throughout the community.	Students update and design your school/district website.
Writing	Students report out on special events like athletic events, recess, show and tell, and more.	Students design a literary magazine that includes student writings, drawing, and artwork.	Students design your school/district weekly newsletter or school newspaper.
Welcome	Students create a video about the school for new students and the community.	Students give tours for all new students.	Students record the welcome message for your phone system, letting callers hear your students voice first.
Video	Students design a short video that is shown to their class.	Students design a documentary shown to the school.	Students design a short feature film shown at your local movie theatre.
Audio	Students lead and announce the morning school announcements.	Students design podcasts on school issues for fellow students.	Students create a podcast that is shared with the community.

We take good notes, a picture of the group, and share it out each week with the students and faculty. During this session, students asked for hot sauce in the cafeteria, paper towels in the bathrooms (we had the high wind hand dryers), a salad bar, and a five-minute extension to school on days with inclement weather. One of my favorite tweets of the school year was when a student took a pic of the hot sauce in the cafe and thanked us for listening. It's hard to believe how the little things make such a huge impact in our schools.

Most recently, the students asked to get additional microwaves in the cafeteria, and they pleaded to remove the ban on bookbags during the school day. Since then, we have started a movement called, "You asked, we listened." We create social media icons, share them out on social media, and generate momentum around what the students are asking for.

What would happen if your school would start a "You Asked, We Listened" campaign to respond to student voice? What would your students ask for, and would you work to make sure their wish comes true?

When students have an opportunity to meet with the school leadership team and express their thoughts on how the school can improve, action must be taken, or trust is broken. You must take action to make the changes recommended or to improve the school like the students suggested. By doing this, you lead the school through the voice of students and empower them to get involved in leadership, not just in the school but after they graduate.

We are continuing to look for ways to improve our school through the lens of students. This can't be accomplished if we don't have a systematic approach to listening to students.

STUDENT CHOICE

In an effort to look for ways to provide students choice in our school, we decided to allow seniors to choose their lockers before school starts. We opened up the school, set up check-in stations in the lobby, and established a procedure for seniors to come in and select the lockers of their choice. By doing this, students gain buy-in and ownership in their school experience.

Providing a range of seating options and allowing students to choose the places they use for their learning is another way to honor student choice. Offer a variety of low desks, standard desks, stools, lounge chairs, folding chairs, web chairs, bean bag chairs, and laptop desks . . . the options are plentiful and affordable. By allowing students to choose the way they would like to sit, stand, or recline while doing their reading, writing, reflecting, and collaborating, we are keeping a focus on what matters most—the learning. We need to give away the power and stop striving for conformity and order above learning.

String Theory School, in our home city of Philadelphia, takes choice to an entirely new level. This school is set up to provide students choice in their learning. String Theory understands that when students are excited about their learning, achievement flourishes. Students get to select how they want to start their learning for the day by selecting from any of the following majors: ballet and Broadway, digital design and fine arts, innovations in science and technology in STEM and engineering/robotics, vocal and instrumental music, theatre and television broadcast arts, and creative writing and digital publishing. We have had the privilege of visiting String Theory to learn about the tremendous opportunities and choice that students are given in their learning. String students need to learn about the core subjects of math, science, history, and English, but they spend a larger amount of time per class in their choice of major. When ballet students know that school starts off with a focus on dance and ballet, they are more likely to get to school on time and to be ready to learn the rest of the day. While at String Theory, students shared with me how they love the opportunity to learn in the area they are most passionate about.

School Showcase

Allowing for Student Choice

School Leader: Jennifer Frantz

Lower Elementary School

New Hope-Solebury School District

As the principal of the Lower Elementary School, a K–2 building in the New Hope-Solebury School District, I encourage teachers to take the risk of allowing student choice within the classroom. In the elementary world, student choice finds the most success when it is married to good classroom management skills, explored expectations, and the ability to find the calm within the chaos. In the following, you will find a menu of options to allow for student choice. I will take a deeper dive into two of the options.

Flexible Seating: Offering an array of options as part of a sensory diet for kids can go a long way! Bucket seats, bean bag chairs, exercise balls, standing desks . . . the choices are limitless.

Genius Hour: Every student has their genius. How do we realize that in our elementary classrooms? Working with students to unearth their passions and what excites them is just one way our teachers encourage students to take ownership of their learning. We offer time during Flex Fridays for students to explore their own wonderings using resources like Ralph Fletcher's *The Writer's Notebook* and A. J. Juliani's book, *Launch.*

Project Based Learning: A new commitment for our teachers this year! In direct collaboration with The Buck Institute and inspired by Ross Cooper and Erin Murphy's book, *Hacking PBL,* our LES teachers are diving into Project Based Learning. The opportunities for choice and problem solving are endless as students work through the design-thinking process. Asking questions, creating problems, and embracing the process of inquiry (over the product!) will be a main focus for our youngest learners this year!

Assignments: Is there an opportunity to offer choice in the order in which students complete tasks or assignments? Some students love doing the more challenging tasks first and saving the "best for last." Others find comfort and confidence in tackling the known before the unknown. This is such a simple way for students to have ownership over their day and can help solve problems before they even start.

Class Meetings: Looking for a time to involve your students in upcoming decisions in the classroom? Class meetings are a great time to garner your students' thoughts, concerns, and praise in order to dig deeper into what makes each unique class tick. Pose questions. Ask for honesty. Build trust, and take student suggestions. Carving out a place to discuss student choice is often the most important step in creating voice in the classroom.

As I mentioned earlier, student choice can be organic in our youngest learning environments, but it can also be terrifying at first. How do I keep all of the students engaged when they are doing different things? How do I hold them accountable? Isn't it too chaotic to have student choice in an elementary classroom? How do I move from an instructor to a facilitator in my own classroom? And the one no one likes to admit: how do I give up control when that's what keeps my learning environment running smoothly?

These are all good, honest, real questions. And they should be asked. Discussed. Dissected. Change is hard for anyone, and it is even harder if it is not prepared for as much as possible. So let's break down how we allow for student choice at the elementary level without overwhelming our teachers—and our students.

First, it is important to know that student choice is not an all-or-nothing phenomenon. Give yourself permission to release control and open up choices slowly. In regard to flexible seating, perhaps only allow student choice during centers at first. Graduate to allowing more choices during direct instruction or even be so bold as to eventually allow your students to set up the room on the first day of school instead of setting it up before they arrive! Don't worry if you need more control over choice than your grade partner or the teacher in the next wing . . . the important part is you're taking a risk to allow for student choice in some way. As you become more comfortable with the gray, you will allow yourself to embrace the opportunity to make the students' voices as powerful—or perhaps even more powerful—than your own.

Second, clear, consistent, communicated expectations are the best friend of student choice. Let's go back to flexible seating. Are you worried everyone will want the same pink chair? Are you picturing students rolling away on exercise balls instead of using them wisely?

(Continued)

(Continued)

Set yourself—and your students—up for success by communicating the perimeters in which flex seating can be used. If every student has a number in your class, perhaps cycle through who gets first choice of the flex seating on a weekly basis. Pair visual and verbal directions on what it looks like to use each flex seating option safely. Explain why it is important to treat all classroom materials with kindness so they can be around to provide options for learners for years to come. There is a place for direct instruction on how to use the flex seating options within a classroom. Don't be afraid to model your expectations and reteach those who need reminders, as necessary. There are so many great ideas for exploring this flex seating on Twitter. Check out @cblitoub (Miss Lindsay Toub, first grade teacher, Central Bucks School District) and any of our teachers at the Lower Elementary School as they explore this opportunity for student choice this year (@FirstGradeLES, @SecondGradeNHS, @KindergartenNHS).

This year we are embracing project-based learning (PBL). We are valuing process over product and embracing the following driving question: How can we plan effective projects for our students? PBL is a choice-based approach to learning and establishing norms, and creating an intentional process helps teachers move from directing all of the information to embracing the idea of becoming the "guide on the side"! One of the most exciting parts of offering student choice at the elementary level is that it also provides opportunities to embrace failure. When students own their own learning and are excited about exploring topics of interest, failure doesn't become an obstacle. . . . it becomes a path to new learning and a true lesson in grit and resilience. We are excited to go on this journey together as a staff this year and look forward to our students guiding the way!

Jennifer Frantz
@jenn_frantz
Principal
Lower Elementary School
New Hope-Solebury School District

Promoting Student Voice

Nancy Alvarez, Principal—Robin Sherwood, Kindergarten @rswd53

Celina Primary School

Celina Independent School District

Teacher Robin Sherwood shares how her class and the school are working to promote student voice.

We want to give opportunity to the students, and we want to say yes as much as possible. We work to use choice cards to provide students the opportunity to choose what they want to learn. Seesaw is an excellent tool that we use to empower student learning. I create a project in Seesaw and attach a video that has my instructions on it, and then the students can do their own differentiation. They respond by writing me a story, recording a video, or drawing a picture. I will ask them to tell me about apples or the numbers to 10, and then they get to complete the task as they want.

Our philosophy is to create authentic, real-life experiences for students. We bring the community in to see and experience learning alongside us. We work to get the community involved as much as we can. For example, I had a parent, who is a judge, come in and share with students about what it means to be a judge.

I give them many, many, many opportunities to speak up and to share what they are learning in the classroom.

With choice, the students know we have flexibility to learn. I need to provide opportunities for innovation and open thinking where they can think up things they want to work on. I give them 20 to 30 minutes at the end of the day when they work on a project that they are passionate about. This causes them to grow as learners and to be independent in their thinking. I had a student create constellations, using the Seesaw app, to build maps of what he sees up in the sky. He would go home and look for those constellations he saw in the sky. He didn't understand the constellations were created hundreds of years ago, but this got him into astronomy and learning about the constellations. We had students who got into broadcasting little videos to express themselves and to share the learning they had with their classmates.

(Continued)

(Continued)

As a leader, Nancy pushes me to challenge myself and to be a leader. She wants me to start striving for more. Nancy leads in a way that creates a culture where I feel safe to be creative and innovative. Unleashing student voice is a tremendous way to improve your school, we don't want to exclude the voice of others. While you're empowering students remember to also share power for decision making with your professional staff. Include them in the student roundtables, and solicit their input on the issues faced by your school community. When leaders share power the whole learning community wins (Ziegler & Ramage, 2012).

HERO SIGHTING

John Hattie refers to an Australian study that concluded, "Rather than being a harmless fad, learning styles theory perpetuates the very stereotyping and harmful teaching practices that it is said to combat" (Hattie & Yates, 2014, p.183).

Reflect with your team. How are you including students' interests in your curriculum, instruction, and assessment practices? What are you doing to ensure students' strengths are being leveraged for their academic success?

Don't confuse teachers' plans to approach learning from a variety of styles (with experiences they choose) with a connection to a student's unique interest and connection to personal prior knowledge. Varied approaches to learning based on readiness and assessment options are both good ideas—but giving students as much autonomy as you can in the learning connected to your core goals is a stronger option. Look over your lessons or district curriculum to see where student voice and choice can be leveraged for greater learning outcomes.

HERO TRAINING

Use these activities to nurture your skills. Even better—gather with your team to embed these skills in your work and empower your students to become heroes that change their world.

1. Use our four survey questions from Figure 4.5, Falcon Feedback Friday Questions, or create your own, and gather a small focus group of students every Friday to ask them. Spend time listening, and then gather your leadership team to discern where those quick wins can be found. Determine the places where student voice can have an immediate impact, and then make sure it does!
2. Work as a team to complete the reflections outlined in figures in this chapter.
3. Visit our website at www.chaselearning.org/herobuilding, and take the Student Voice and Choice survey to see how your team is doing in promoting student voice and choice in your school.
4. Empower students to lead a faculty/staff meeting or student assembly program.

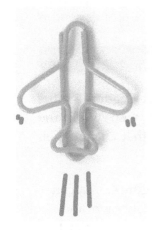

LEAD LIKE AN ALIEN

Out of This World Ideas to Produce Hero Students

"Even if you're on the right track, you'll get run over if you just sit there."

—Will Rogers

[Dave] When I first started learning to ride a motorcycle, I spent time reading through all kinds of safety manuals and training materials. In some ways, it was like riding any other two-wheeled vehicle I had experienced as a kid, but in other ways, it was a completely unknown and unfamiliar experience. After doing hours of classroom work, it was time to get on the road and start to hone my skills. My comfort level, and proficiency, was growing with the effort I dedicated to this new pursuit. One of the key events that boosted my comfort and skills considerably in this early stage was learning about counter steering. In a car, steering initiates turning. On a motorcycle, lean angle initiates turning, and to accomplish this, we need counter steering.

At the core of this concept is a very alien idea—to get the motorcycle to go left you must first turn right.

This is true for any two-wheeled vehicle; however, the process is masked when you try it at speeds of less than eight or nine miles per hour. Especially at highway speeds, the way a motorcycle changes direction relies on the effects of counter steering. Some riding instructors even use a one-handed exercise that has riders "pushing" the handlebars away instead of what we all think about the "pulling" the handlebars toward the turn. I'm not a physicist, but I know that something amazing is going on here, and I've experienced it. If I would try to keep the mindset of a car driver (or slow speed two-wheeled driver), the results would be disastrous. The reminder? Be open to new ideas, even radical ideas, to accomplish your work. What could be a more basic skill on a motorcycle than turning? And what could be a more radical realization than it starts by going the wrong way?

We challenge school leaders to think differently so we can learn to lead more effectively. Let's explore out-of-this-world ideas that may be alien to our thinking and practices. These alien ideas have a research base, but it's been too easy for school leaders to default to the ineffective ideas of schooling that we experienced ourselves as we journeyed through our educational experiences. Unknowingly, many leadership mentors may have added to this problem. Instead, we want to encourage the eyes of a foreigner, or alien, a fresh vision that will unlock the "Area 51 of School Leadership" for topics we rarely question or consider the efficacy of in practice. These ideas may be foreign to many, but they will really work to prepare our kids for a world that is complex and changing. We will show how these ideas are not like the little green people that inhabit a faraway planet but rather real, practical, and research-based ideas that lead students to becoming powerful heroes ready to take on the challenges of our world.

Sometimes the ideas that transform our leadership practices are ideas that come from a discipline outside our own (Johansson, 2017). Powerful outcomes sometimes emerge from very different components that bring a surprising complement to each other. Johansson talks about the impractical, burdensome situation for women wearing burkas who want to swim with their young children. An innovative thinker pondered the situation, observed a wide variety of female swimmers, and developed the burkini—a modest suit that honored the design of the burka, yet benefited from the wicking power of a fabric more well-suited for swimming. The result was a product that couldn't be produced fast enough! This is not primarily a story about business success, it's a story that transformed the experience for these new moms and their young children. This inventor is a hero for these moms. Where are the next, discrepant ideas that might provide a powerful synergy for our work as leaders? The following are some of our out-of-this-world ideas for you to consider for your own leadership work.

BREAK DOWN HISTORICAL BARRICADES

We are not talking about breaking through the locks of Area 51 or landing a spaceship on Mars, although that would be really cool. We are talking about breaking down the barriers and barricades that educators have historically built to keep students contained. It's time that we shatter the boundaries and provide students with opportunities for growth and progress. We are talking about prerequisites on courses, age limits for activities, or standard protocol that schools have put in place for years to serve as barriers for kids to move to the next level. We have gotten really good at creating barriers in schools to make learning and school easier on the adults rather than more challenging and empowering for the students. It's time we shatter these boundaries to allow students the ability to lead in a way that our world notices. Consider two common ways your school may be forcing barriers and unnecessary boundaries on

> We need to break down boundaries around courses that keep the average student out and allow only the highest achievers in.

@DrBillZiegler @DrDaveRamage

kids trying to enroll in your "preferred courses" within their program of studies.

Prerequisites for Courses. Many schools place boundaries around courses keeping the average student out and allowing only the highest achievers in. What does this do to empower students? Nothing. It simply teaches kids they aren't good enough to reach a goal or challenge themselves to a higher level of learning. Worst of all, it teaches them they don't belong in those courses. These boundaries also create an equity issue. We challenge you to walk in your honors and upper level courses and look at the demographics. Do the demographics of those classes reflect your school community? Is there a proportional number of economically disadvantaged students, is the population as diverse as your school, and does it reflect balance in gender? For the most part, prerequisites are designed for the adults, not the students. It's time we release our students to new challenges and reexamine why we have prerequisites and what we are doing to make sure all students have equal opportunities.

Leaders need to break down the walls and barriers that are holding students back from reaching high and achieving their dreams. We can do this by providing additional supports for students to take challenging courses, implementing interventions that are personalized and strategic, and ensuring that the mindsets of faculty and staff are committed to the success of every child. Leaders need to closely monitor these practices to ensure that all students are given opportunities to grow and achieve.

Work Habits for Courses. In most cases, the prerequisites are not the only hurdle in place for our students. We even devise systems where a high-achieving student may not get the opportunity to enter an accelerated course because he or she is not seen as a student who has the study skills or work ethic to keep up in a fast-paced environment. Why don't we share clear expectations, allow willing learners to enter the class, expect their success, and set up supports so anyone who struggles can receive targeted remediation to achieve at his or her highest level? Instead of corralling the most compliant and historically high-achieving students in one space and perpetuating their label, let's get more students involved with our most intense, authentic, relevant, and rewarding learning experiences. Is this an alien idea in your setting?

PROCRASTINATORS PRODUCE

[Bill] Growing up, I was the ultimate procrastinator, and my teachers would regularly warn me that this would catch up to me someday. They were right. It caught up to me as I found some of my best work at the last minute, in the darkness of night before writing my dissertation, or moments before walking on stage to speak to thousands. I have generated some of my best work when I was forced to come up with a resolution and when I was under mild stress at the last minute. You see, as educators, we tend to believe that everything must be organized nicely, prepared well in advance, and written on notecards to find true success.

This concept of procrastinators produce is definitely an out-of-this-world idea and mindset for educators. It has been drilled into us that procrastination is a bad thing and that it only leads to sloppy work or no work at all. The alien thinking of procrastinators produce supports students and allows them to be creative, think outside the box, and challenge the status quo.

University of Pennsylvania Professor and best-selling author Adam Grant shares in his research that even Dr. Martin Luther King was revising and adding to his "I Have a Dream" speech while sitting on stage. He shares observations of politician Drew Hansen, who shared, "Just before King spoke," he was "crossing out lines and scribbling new ones as he awaited his turn," and "it looked like King was still editing his speech until he walked to the podium to deliver it" (Grant, 2016, pp. 101–102). Schools, and many leaders, teach that procrastination is a bad habit that we need to break. But have we considered that procrastination can actually lead to powerful creativity and innovation? Check out our website at www .chaselearning.org/herobuilding for a powerful video from Penn professor Adam Grant on the power of procrastination.

Perhaps procrastination empowers students rather than hurts them. When we procrastinate, we are often more creative and focused because we know there's a looming deadline. The professional development blog at Harvard University's Extension School states,

> For the procrastinators in our midst who often succumb to deadline-induced stress, it may be surprising to discover that procrastination has its advantages. Procrastination gives you time to consider divergent ideas, to think in nonlinear ways, and to make unexpectant leaps. (Leslie, 2017)

Creativity thrives on the incubation of ideas instead of the quick fix of the first solution that comes to mind (Dacey & Lennon, 1998). Not everything can, or should, wait until the last minute, but don't underestimate the power of procrastination. Maybe it's an idea whose time has come for your organization? (Don't answer right away, think about it for a while before you respond.)

BELLS ARE BARRIERS

Why do we drive our regular school day by the bell? We can actually trace the answer to that question back to an earlier time in our American school systems. Way back, actually, to 1893 when educational leaders gathered and anticipated the economy would change in our society from agrarian to industrial. This Committee of Ten worked to change schools from one-room schoolhouses to a factory model (Dintersmith, 2018). The school bell rings, and learning stops for three minutes as students pass in the halls or run to recess. Sure, we know that many companies in the 1950s were driven by the ringing of the break or lunch bell, but today our workplaces are much more complex and less dependent on stopping when the bell rings. How can we rethink learning with regard to time, and how can school leaders strengthen learning by using time to their advantage?

Another of the negative outcomes of bell-driven days is the way disciplines have become extremely compartmentalized. You have surely heard the story of a science teacher who complains that students lack a basic math skill, yet those same students demonstrate mastery of that exact skill during math class, right before their science period, in a room immediately across the hallway.

We encourage leaders to closely examine if their school schedule supports or detracts from learning. Block scheduling, flexible scheduling, "Genius Hour" blocks of time, and alternating daily schedules are all ways that can support extended learning blocks to foster greater time for learning.

How can we take the lessons of Genius Hour, FedEx, Unconferences, and EdCamps to find ways to use time more fluidly and flexibly during our school day? Office hours in Schoology, Remind™ sessions, or Twitter Chat study sessions are all ways to leverage technology to create time and space for continued learning. The time has come to break free from the factory model. In our secondary schools, it's always powerful to consider ways to do cross-curricular work, especially with interdisciplinary team projects and instruction.

> We must grade differently from the way we were graded. We need to create new grading practices that prepare students for success.
>
> @DrBillZiegler @DrDaveRamage

GRADES MATTER MOST

If you want to talk about an area that is foreign and out of this world for many, it's grading. We grade the same way we were graded and continue to perpetuate grading practices that were handed down through generations, like the story of grandpa seeing that spaceship over the mountain on his way home from watching the Twilight Zone. These grading practices are not based on research or best practice but rather what worked for us, our parents, and our grandparents. It's time we reexamine the green glob in the alien world of grading. We need to shift the emphasis from grading to learning. We need to examine the purpose of grading. The time-honored way we approach grades is designed to sort students. Parents simply want to know, "How does my child stack up against the others?" The out-of-this-world thinking around grading shifts the primary purpose of grading to feedback for the learners and the teacher. If aliens observed our grading practices, they'd be inclined to wonder why we surprise learners with material we haven't taught and wonder why many don't succeed on exams.

As educators, we have gotten sucked into the vortex of believing that grading is vital in learning and school. But reality is just the opposite; grading doesn't score mastery, it doesn't show a student's ability or talents, and it certainly doesn't determine future success. Yet, we continue to hold to the practice of grading everything without fully understanding what research says about grading. The subjectivity of teacher grading is not brought into question, many schools never discuss best practices in regard to teaching, and many teachers are still grading just the way their teachers graded years, or decades, ago.

Grades help perpetuate the thinking that educators select talent rather than develop it. By allowing this thinking to persist, we hurt students and cause them to believe that their failures hold them back. Along-the-way grades should be more like the design failures, and iterations, that eventually help inform a successful design or performance.

Alfie Kohn (1999) weighs in with research on the effects of grading and finds three consistent effects of using, and especially emphasizing, the importance of number or letter grades. One is grades tend to reduce students' interest in the learning itself. A second is grades tend to reduce students' preference for challenging tasks. And a third is grades reduce the quality of students' thinking. Toss in the reality that classroom grading practices lack statistical reliability and validity, and the quagmire of grading issues seems to grow and grow (Wormeli, 2018).

We aren't going to dig deeply into grading practices, but we do want to leave you with thoughts to consider from author and educator Rich Wormeli. He shares ten grading practices that all educators should avoid in his latest book, *Fair Isn't Always Equal*, second edition (2018).

1. Incorporating nonacademic factors such as behavior, attendance, and effort into the academic report of standards/outcomes, that is, the grade or percentage on the report card
2. Penalizing students' multiple attempts at mastery
3. Grading practice (homework)
4. Withholding assistance
5. Assessing students in ways that do not accurately indicate their mastery
6. Allowing extra credit and bonus points to change the grade report
7. Using a group grade to assess any one student on the standard
8. Grading on a curve
9. Using nonreferenced terms to describe criterion-referenced attributes
10. Recording zeros on the 100-point scale for work not done

If you scored a 20 to 24 on Figure 5.1, you are a grading rockstar who is well on your way to grading kids for what really counts. If your score is between 16 and 19, you are making great progress, but we would challenge you to dig into best practices in grading and look for ways to make systemic shifts in grading throughout your school culture. If you scored 10 to 15, you have some work to do in regard to learning about best grading practices. We would encourage you to connect with us to learn how we are shifting grading practices in our

Figure 5.1   Grading Reflection Tool

Question	Infrequently (1)	Sometimes (2)	Regularly (3)	Always (4)
Homework is not graded.				
Nonacademic indicators are not counted or separated from the grade (lateness, neatness, word counts, etc.).				
If using a 10-point scale, a 0 is never given.				
Extra credit is not permitted.				
Students are given multiple attempts at mastery.				
Individual grades are given during group work.				

schools to grade what really counts. If you scored 6 to 9, it's time to start now in learning about best practices in grading, examining your school's current grading structure, and working to align it to best practices. This will take courage and a tireless commitment, but it will pay off huge dividends for your kids as they grow and become successful in learning. Connect with us to learn about our story on how we are working to shift grading practices to strengthen learning and growth for kids.

REPETITION IS WRONG

One of the most time-honored strategies a teacher will use to help a student with study skills is, "Read the chapter again." While close reading is a strategy that can produce benefits, particularly after the first reading of a passage, the rereading strategy is ineffective for learning that will stick with the student. Brown, Roediger, and McDaniel discovered that "doing multiple readings in close succession is a time-consuming strategy that yields negative benefits at the expense of much more effective strategies that take less time" (2014, p. 261). It turns out learning is an acquired skill, and some of the most effective strategies will be counterintuitive to our own history of learning experiences.

Clearly there are times when rereading a section of text is absolutely needed to build understanding. What we need to avoid is the notion that effective studying for an assessment includes the default advice to "read the chapter again and pay attention to your notes and outlines." In reality, this is just another cramming strategy that emphasizes getting information into your head when the real key to learning is building strong pathways to access the multitude of information we already have to get it out.

[Dave] Reading *Make It Stick* (Brown et al., 2014) was a great reminder for me to remember what our profession has gained in our understanding about learning. The many advances in neuroscience over the past two decades should lead to a change in our practices as educators and leaders. One area that most classrooms are guilty of engaging in is the practice that neuroscientists identify as "massed practice." One common example of massed practice is cramming for an exam. While most teachers would recommend looking over material for a longer period of time than the night before, they are still often guilty of using massed practice in their instruction. Let me give you an example that I'm sure you've experienced yourself.

In math class you probably learned the formula for computing the volume of a cylinder. You talked about it, watched a teacher model the use of the formula, and then practiced with a number of problems on your own (probably something like numbers 1 through 30 but only the odd numbers—math teachers love that kind of homework). After a lesson or two, you learned that computing the volume for a conical shape is a little different. This led to a new formula, modeling by the teacher, and a new set of odd-numbered or even-numbered problems to tackle for homework. After a lesson or two with this new skill, you learned how to find the volume of an irregular shaped object. This was yet another formula, modeling, and practice on your own. Seems like a great way to systematically learn about volume, right?

The description of math learning you just read is a classic example of massed practice. Get one thing, and repeat it over and over, then go to the next thing, and so on. Practice that one thing over and over (massed) until you master it. The really nefarious part of this equation (pun intended) is that mass practice gives you the false sense of really learning something deeply. You make quick headway with the skill, and it seems like you really know it. The problem comes when we check to see if it's learning that really sticks with you. Weeks or months later when you are asked to work with volume of objects, it's likely that the massed practice is no longer easily accessed and recalled.

A much stronger approach to learning comes in the use of spaced practice (Brown et al., 2014; Hattie & Yates, 2014).

Spaced practice is the opposite of cramming. In the math example, it's about learning the three types of shapes, with associated formulas, but keeping them all on the table simultaneously. Ideally, you would also toss in some problems and formulas from previous units of study. By returning to skills and concepts that we've addressed in earlier learning, we are forcing the brain to "find that information" again. This retrieving of information is really the key to strong learning. It's not about dumping information into the brain—that's the easy part. In fact, we could argue that we have as much information as we want at our fingertips, or keystrokes. In reality, what we have is information overload, whether we want it or not. So, if learning is not about dumping information in, what is it about? Getting information out.

Spaced practice helps our brain build, and strengthen, the pathways needed to get our learning out when we need it. There is no doubt that this kind of practice can be harder and more frustrating. But each time we have a productive struggle to find that learning from the past, we make it easier to access that learning the next time. We know that activating prior knowledge is a powerful part of learning. In simple terms, it helps us build a path back to our new learning because we attach it with something already established. Repetition is needed in learning, but the kind of repetition we traditionally provide (massed practice) is the wrong kind of repetition. Space out your practice instead.

TRADITION HOLDS US DOWN

Ask most school leaders and teachers how they came up with their grading practices, philosophy of being a school leader, how to run a school, or what a school should look like, and most would tell you something very similar—that they learned through what they experienced as a student or what other teachers/school leaders have shown them. These approaches are not based in best practice, research, or data that focus on how to improve schools and prepare kids for the complex and changing needs in our world. The alien approach can show us how to keep the good, let go of the bad, and pull ahead of the past to prepare our kids for their unknown future.

Alien eyes, fresh eyes, in our leadership contexts can help us see the culture that we take for granted. Seymour Sarason (1996) reminds us that truly productive learning is characterized by students who walk away from the experience wanting to learn more. If this is true, we don't need alien eyes to see that most of our programs are failing miserably. Is it possible to take radical approaches and bring them to scale in our large public school settings? It's sure worth trying! Public schools like Clairemont Elementary School in Decatur, GA; Grand Rapids Public Museum School in Grand Rapids, MI; Lake View High School in Chicago, IL; MAST Academy in Key Biscayne, FL; Quest To Learn in New York, NY; Vail Ski & Snowboard Academy in Vail, CO; and the Zoo School in Grand Rapids, MI were all highlighted for innovative, out-of-this-world approaches to learning (Noodle, 2015). Resist the lie that says innovative learning success is only for a small, private, well-funded schools. Do you believe your own school can reinvent itself in big and small ways that benefit your students? Resist the pull of tradition, and rise above the strong voice of "We've always done it this way."

HOMEWORK HELPS

When we start rethinking homework, we begin to push at one of the most time-honored, unquestioned aspects of teaching and learning. Most educators will swear by not only its academic effectiveness but also the way it "prepares students for the real world." Fortunately, certain educational leaders have proven to hold the role of "alien voice" more than others, and in this uncommon world, few scholars have filled the role with as much insight, thoughtfulness, poignancy, and style as

Alfie Kohn. He is arguably education's most outspoken critic about our schools' fixation on grading policies and standardized test scores.

With regard to how schools view homework Kohn (2006) shares,

> In short, regardless of one's criteria, there is no reason to think that most students would be at any sort of disadvantage if homework were sharply reduced or even eliminated. Nevertheless, the overwhelming majority of American schools—elementary and secondary, public and private—continue to require their students to work a second shift by bringing academic assignments home.

Kohn also concludes there isn't a shred of evidence to support the assumption that homework produces nonacademic benefits for students of any age.

In Chapter 2, we read about Alfonz and the reasons why homework wasn't a viable part of his daily routines. To paraphrase Kohn's observation, Alfonz already had a second shift. When homework is given, it almost always connects with another problem we just discussed—massed practice. Very rarely have I seen a homework assignment that intentionally recycles skills and concepts that have been mastered during an earlier unit of study to keep them fresh and introduce spaced practice opportunities for students.

This will be a difficult conversation with many of your faculty members, but it may be time to make homework disappear. We took an intermediary step in Pottsgrove School District some years ago, but it's a move in the right direction. Following the lead of many of our most successful teachers, we suggested homework be greatly reduced (or eliminated) and not be graded. We also set a maximum percentage of a students' grade that could be determined by homework when it was used in formative grading. This helped bring equity in grading across classrooms with disparate homework policies and patterns. This also helped us gauge a more accurate picture of what a classroom grade meant in terms of mastery of core skills and concepts—especially for students like Alfonz. Can your school examine the role of homework and make some out-of-this-world changes that will benefit your students?

A type of homework that really helps and strengthens kids is reading. When kids find a love of reading things they enjoy, they become stronger thinkers, writers, and learners. For many, this is a missing piece in the lives of our kids. By helping them find a love of reading, we empower them to be lifelong learners who can think critically, analyze information, and dream up solutions to today's real-world problems. How awesome would it be if every educator was committed to frequently assigning reading for pleasure as a homework assignment? Books are life changing, and now more than ever, students can have access to the world's greatest libraries right on their phones. Providing books at various reading levels, developing a strong reading program in your school, and being focused on developing a love of reading should be a core mission for every leader.

THINK DIFFERENTLY

The story of Hugh Thompson during the Vietnam War is an example of a shift in thinking that certainly has serious consequences. It literally centers on life and death outcomes. We bring it up in our discussion of out-of-this-world ideas because it was so unlike the climate and culture Hugh found himself in, yet he was willing to see, think, and act in a better way. His story is embedded in the tragedy of the My Lai Massacre.

In March of 1968, Thompson and his two-man flight crew saved Vietnamese civilians by personally escorting them away from advancing United States Army ground units and assuring their safe evacuation by air. Thompson was an Army helicopter pilot. Thompson radioed several times to alert operational headquarters about the danger these innocent civilians found themselves in as U.S. troops were approaching. When no action was taken, Thompson reported again that a massacre was occurring. A lieutenant colonel eventually ordered all ground units to cease the search and destroy operations in this village (Weiner, 2018).

Before the killing stopped, U.S. Army ground units were looking for Viet Cong fighters, but in the air, Thompson was noticing large numbers of bodies below him. The bodies were old men, old women, children, and babies, not combatants. Initially, he couldn't understand what was happening on the ground—his thinking wouldn't allow it. When he broke away from the core beliefs and culture that was so embedded in the paradigm of this honorable band of brothers, he finally admitted to himself that he was witnessing an atrocity beyond his comprehension.

He and his crew continued to put themselves in danger to rescue the wounded and transport them to hospitals. Thompson had heated exchanges with some of the U.S. soldiers in the ground troops before operational headquarters eventually called off the operation. When Thompson returned to the base, he filed a formal complaint.

After the complaint, the Army tried to cover up what had happened at My Lai. Eventually, a journalist, Seymour Hersh, found out about the massacre and made it worldwide news. Thompson testified against the commanding officer at the time of the massacre. The backlash toward Thompson from the Army was harsh. He didn't have support for decades despite the fact that he continued to serve diligently. Thirty years later, the U.S. Army acknowledged that Thompson had done something good. In 1998, they awarded him the Soldier's Medal for heroism not involving actual conflict with the enemy. On the 30th anniversary of the massacre, Thompson returned to My Lai and met some of the people whose lives he had saved (Weiner, 2018).

We know Americans committed a massacre almost 51 years ago during the ravages of war. We also know that one American stopped it. Hugh Thompson is a hero that thought differently than the status quo he found himself placed in, and thank goodness he did. Your school is not a battleground for life and death, but if we fail in our calling to equip students with the skills they need, we are certain to diminish the quality of their current, and future, lives. What is happening in the classrooms and hallways around you that needs a new direction? What new thinking is required to re-engage students and families in the learning that can literally change their lives? What new thinking is required to take your teachers and students to the next level? How can you work to strengthen learning and build culture in your school? Think differently!

We have all heard the quote by Albert Einstein, "The definition of insanity is doing the same thing over and over and expecting different results." We can go insane spinning our wheels around the same ideas and thinking as leaders in schools and districts. To change this thinking, we challenge you to do these four things:

1. Visit Schools—We learn so much when we visit other schools. We are always finding ourselves writing things down or taking pictures to use in our school.
2. Read Research and Best Practices—It's so easy to get sucked into simply learning from social media, but sometimes that can perpetuate bad practices. Take time to read about "best practices" and research in learning. Dig into what the latest research is saying about learning, building culture, and leading.
3. Build a Professional Learning Network—Build a strong support network that will challenge your thinking and push you beyond the status quo. This can be a group in your school, district, or anywhere in the world.
4. Wear Your Watch on the Opposite Hand You Normally Do—Motivational speaker Simon Bailey challenged me [Bill] and a group of leaders to change the way we wear our watch for one day as a reminder of how we need to stretch beyond our own comfort levels to grow. I struggled with this, it was uncomfortable to switch wrists, but I found myself using it as a reminder to stretch myself to grow.

You are the educational leader. You are the person needed to step in and change the learning to support the students you serve. Despite any backlash or exclusion you may experience, don't be the commander who keeps the wrong action occurring over and over again. Be the leader who steps up to do the right thing regardless of the resistance you might face. Be strong and courageous. You'll learn about resistance in the next chapter and gain some tools to push back for what matters most. And, don't tackle this most important mission alone, build a team around you that champions the cause of kids in a powerful and meaningful way.

Leading like an alien isn't easy, but it is worth it to provide students with an out-of-this-world learning environment. We challenge you to consider what areas of your thinking or practice need to be challenged and reexamined. Consider which foreign idea we shared resonates with you the most. It's time to shatter the status quo and to lead in a way that is backed by research and best practice. By doing this, you prepare your students for a complex and changing world.

HERO SIGHTING

"People have great difficulty in benchmarking the notion of 'average.' But whatever this average is, we all know that we are a great deal better" (Hattie & Yates, 2014, p. 229).

Reflect with your team. How will you work as a leadership team to help students, and fellow staff members, gain an accurate picture of their strengths? What are the data available to help guide these conversations? Is there an inventory of strengths you can use to describe a more accurate picture for self-reflection?

This finding from Hattie's work can be a stinging reminder that we may not possess the individual expertise as educators and leaders that we think. More importantly, it's a reminder to be sure we are checking for students' understanding and growth in accurate ways. This does not mean only quantitative data count! In fact, we're encouraging you to go in the other direction and be sure to gather qualitative data to share with your students. This is a reminder that individual student conferencing provides an opportunity for a learning conversation that provides great insight. This is equally true for leaders and the culture they are building. Whether it's classroom, school, or district, take some time to have a quality conversation with those you are leading, and consider how you can take the next incremental step in your hero-building leadership skills.

HERO TRAINING

Use these activities to nurture your skills. Even better—gather with your team to embed these skills in your work and empower your students to become heroes that change their world.

1. Hero SIM—Work with your leadership team to complete the 5.0 Hero SIM on Leading Like an Alien!! You can find it online at www.chaselearning.org/ herobuilding
2. Gather demographic research about the enrollment in your honors classes so you have data to drive the equity you seek for your students and community. How will you bridge the gaps or celebrate your successes in this area?
3. Which ideas challenged your thinking the most in this chapter, and how did it cause you to reconsider your current thinking?
4. If you want to learn how procrastination can lead to increased creativity, just wait a little while. Nothing has to be done yet in this area!
5. Reflect on your school's grading practices compared to Wormeli's grading practices to avoid. How does your school match up?

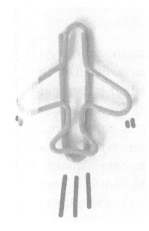

6

BUILD RESILIENCE
Raise Your Grit Score

*"You should never view your challenges as a disadvantage.
Instead, it's important for you to understand that your
experience facing and overcoming adversity is actually one of
your biggest advantages."*

—Michelle Obama

[Bill] I grew up in a loving blue-collar family with parents who were committed to having their kids go to college. My dad was a machinist, and my mom was a stay-at-home mom. Both only had a high school education and dreamed that their children would graduate from college; as a result, when I entered high school, I enrolled in the college preparatory track of classes with a focus on going to college to fulfill my parents' dream. I began to struggle academically in the college prep track, so my parents scheduled a parent teacher conference to learn how they could support me and what I could do to turn my performance around. It was at this conference that I met one of the loudest resistors in my life. I remember this resistor like it was yesterday. At the conference, my dad shared how his boy was going to go off to college, and he inquired how to turn around my performance. While each teacher was reporting out on my achievements, one teacher stopped my dad cold in his tracks. The teacher shared, "Mr. and Mrs. Ziegler, your son is not college material, he will never make it in college!" Although my parents never believed this teacher's judgment, they knew that I could overcome the resistance, but I believed, even internalized, this teacher's belief through years of learning. That year, I received a call from the school after the school year ended and was told that I had failed ninth grade and would need to either repeat the grade or attend summer school. Later in high school, I took the SAT and scored a 660, that's combined on both math and reading. As I read the results, I thought the teacher's judgment of me was right, I thought I was stupid and couldn't make it in college, I wasn't college material. However, my parents constantly reminded me that I was created for greatness and that I would eventually succeed in college. Against my will, my dad enrolled me in Montgomery County Community College and selected courses to start the fall semester. This again was one of those days I'll never forget. My pa made me get in the car, he drove me the 50-minute drive to the community college, and he dropped me off with my schedule in hand. As he pulled away, I turned and just stared at the car crying because I felt like the biggest failure in the world. My dad thought I could go to college, but I barely passed high school. To me, that teacher was right, I wasn't college material. Well, I went to class that day and started a long journey of overcoming several resistors in my learning to earn an associate degree. While earning my degree, I took an education class, and my passion and career choice was ignited. I started seeing myself as a teacher. I went on to earn a bachelor's degree and got a job doing what I never thought was possible. I was a twelfth-grade American Government teacher! As a teacher, my principal encouraged me to earn a master's degree and principal certification. Once I became an administrator, I decided to pursue my doctorate degree. Then, on Thursday, May 20, 2005, I led all Temple

University graduates into commencement and looked over to find my mom and dad crying as they cheered me on. You see, on this day, the resistor was silenced!

All heroes face resistance; it's this resistance that ultimately makes them stronger, challenges them to grow, and improves their own skills. Just like heroes, school leaders can't grow tired of facing the resistance that will come about in their schools. We assure you, there will be resistance throughout your career as a school leader. School leaders and students need to practice the skills of overcoming the naysayers, engaging the resistors, and surmounting the blockades in our life and work. We need to beat the resistance and build support from the opposition. Words like *resistance* and *opposition* may be rough or sound severe, but sugar coating the resistance that school leaders and students face in their journey only serves to minimize the difficulties and trials. We need to build resilience skills to overcome the daily challenges leaders face.

Below are some common resistors that you and students will face through life. As heroes, we need to know, understand, and act to overcome these resistors if we have any hope of being successful. One thing that I love about hero movies is the clearly articulated resistor. The Joker, Cat Woman, Lex Luthor, Darth Vader, and Thanos are just some of the villains that notable heroes have faced on the big screen or in comic books. Unlike these fictitious villains, our resistors are real, right in front of us, and on our team. Resistors can also spread errant beliefs that our team members hold. Who, or what ideas, are resistors, and how do we overcome them?

WHADITW

"We have always done it that way." Those seven words may be the deadliest words for schools, learning, and progress. We Have Always Done It That Way, or as we will refer to it, WHADITW—these iconic words have stopped progress in its tracks and have held schools and their leaders from moving forward. This mantra can frustrate even the most powerful leaders in their work and make them reconsider their purpose and focus. Remember that listening to those with different, even opposing, views can also enrich the solutions we devise.

Leaders can't always steer clear of WHADITW, and when it arrives, we must address it head on. Followers of WHADITW are everywhere and few things can sap a leader's energy like this mentality. The following are some ways leaders can challenge the status quo, overcome WHADITW, and keep their whole community moving forward:

- Build Trust—First and foremost is the importance of building trust. This may require the leader to slow down progress. Even though slowing down the pace of progress may sound counterintuitive, by building trust, the leader establishes a base of trust throughout the organization. Work on building trust first.
- Mission Minded—Keep the school's mission at the forefront, and remind everyone of the goals, vision, mission, and core values. Use these standards to move the organization forward and to challenge the status quo.
- Data Driven—Use data to show the need to move forward and to shatter the status quo. Share how WHADITW is not getting the job done.
- Student Centered—Many times, WHADITW is more for the adults than it is for the students. Sadly, too many schools are designed for the adults rather than the kids. When schools are truly student centered, WHADITW is on the defensive, and progress begins to spread like wild fire.
- Resilience Road Runners—Continue to move forward with resilience. Keep moving down the road of progress, and don't allow the WHADITW mentality to sidetrack you or those in the school.
- Student Feedback—Many times, students challenge WHADITW more than anyone else. They see things from a fresh perspective and new outlook. They understand that progress requires change. Use this feedback to share with the WHADITW believers.

- Courageous Conversations—To shatter the
  WHADITW philosophy, leaders must have courageous
  conversations. These conversations are difficult but
  necessary. Don't take them personally, stick to the facts,
  don't get emotionally charged, and be sure to value
  and respect the person you are conversing with at all
  times. Courageous conversations take place when
  WHADITW is holding back student learning, growth,
  achievement, or progress. There should be no tolerance
  for this type of behavior, it must be addressed with
  kindness, respect, and confidence.

Be sure to answer the WHADITW questions in Figure 6.1
and at the end of this chapter in the Hero Training section.
Take time to reflect on these questions and to see how you can
move beyond the WHADITW in your school.

Figure 6.1   The WHADITW Reflection Tool—Use these prompts to
have conversations that lead to change.

We Have Always Done It That Way – Reflection Questions

PERFECTION BEFORE ACTION?

Striving for perfection can paralyze us, and it often prevents leaders and students from really moving forward. The focus on perfection causes us to work tirelessly and keeps us endlessly hoping to get everything perfect. I don't know why so many leaders are wired for perfection, but this type of wiring can short circuit us and build frustration rather than the optimism and energy required for successful leadership work.

Your students and staff don't need you to be perfect, they need you to be authentic. When we are authentic, we reveal our true identity for our faculty, staff, and students to connect with. None of us are perfect, so stop pretending to be. Allow your students and staff to see that we make mistakes, learn, and adjust. This allows students to see us as learners, as well as leaders. It also frees us from inaction because we know we can take a risk to do what's right, what's needed, and adjust for any improvements or corrections we need after our initial actions.

PUBLIC PRAISER

Sometimes our apparent supporters—those faculty and staff who love our ideas and initiatives when we discuss them in public settings like a large committee or faculty meeting—are the strongest detractors who subtly sabotage the implementation of our work together. They can't wait to break into small groups and tell everyone, "This will never work." Their approach is to divide and conquer. They try to pull the majority of their peers to a position that opposes the goal you have in mind.

The best way to take on these resistors is face first. Go right in, and confront with a respectful and gentle approach. Share with them that you were surprised to hear that they aren't aligning to your mission because you thought they were so supportive. Don't wait or delay, or it will only become more problematic. Plus, this resistor has the chance to grow and multiply quickly. Listen to them and why they oppose the focus, but be sure to let them know that you expect their support in moving forward. Tell them that they are an important part of the team, and their participation is needed to be fully successful. Then, check back and monitor these resistors. If approached properly, we are confident these resistors can become some of your biggest supporters

This Too Will Pass

When I started teaching, I worked for an innovative principal who lived to shatter the status quo and raise achievement for all students. He was passionate, a tireless worker, and visionary in his approach. This didn't sit well with some of my colleagues. I'll never forget sitting in the faculty room and overhearing three of the veterans talking back and forth about the new initiative he put in place. They said something like this, "Hang in there, I've been here 30 years, and this too will pass. I've seen a ton of new initiatives and principals come and go, the principal is just trying to make a name for himself, we will outlive him and this initiative."

The leader must address this indifference in a way that demonstrates care and respect. Many times, these wait-it-out individuals are veterans who are highly respected in the school. They don't typically have ill intent, they are just numb to the never-ending initiatives put upon them through the years. Work to support them as people, listen to their voices, and be patient with them. Show them that you are going to support them, give them the resources to be successful, and follow up to observe progress. Build trust together over time, and this group will go through a wall for you. Your leadership can create a staff full of heroes that will go anywhere and do anything to help their students succeed.

The Distractor

Some people with divergent agendas may have good intentions and correct motives, but their distraction can be a powerful detractor to the work at hand. Others may use distraction as an intentional strategy to derail a leadership direction they oppose. Regardless of the motive, distraction from the core work will draw your attention away from what matters most. It can direct your attention to problems that consume your time. It can paralyze an organization by pointing out the weak areas of the school and constantly harping on them without bringing solutions.

Even the well-intended resistor may come to you with numerous ideas that don't align to your school's mission and focus, and this will sap your energy or cause you to bounce around losing focus and attention. I've fallen prey to this resistor trying to support what is good but not on mission, chasing the wind on something that consumed my time or diverted from the school and district mission, vision, and core values in order to support a teacher. These distractions that come with good intentions are the most difficult to say no to because you really want to support the people and their ventures; however, it's important to weigh the costs and to examine if this will grow students and the school.

Wow, we find distraction to be some of the most difficult resistance because it can easily get us off track and out of focus. With this kind of resistor, it's important to have a clear picture, direction, mission, and focus in your approach. Remind someone of this when they bring you a distraction. Ask questions like, "How does this fit into our school's mission?", "How will this support our goals?", or "Where do you see this fitting into the fabric of the school community?" When supported and redirected, this group of resistors can become as powerful as the Avengers or the Justice League, they just need a hero like you to redirect them.

THE OVERBEARING OCTOPUS

We used the metaphor of an octopus because these resistors can come in and wrap their tentacles around you so tightly that you are literally choked out. The overbearing octopus will consume your time, resources, and energy. And they will cause you to doubt your mission and focus. These are the resistors that grill you with questions in front of an audience like a faculty meeting, are constantly in your office or on the phone ranting and screaming at you about their cause, or writing incessant e-mails that are the longer than the book *War and Peace*.

Sometimes the best offense is a great defense. As Casey Stengel liked to point out, "The key to being a good manager is keeping the people who hate me away from those who are still undecided." A great defense—being willing to be patient, reflect, and pause instead of plowing ahead—can help create a culture that keeps resistors from gaining a foothold. Many times, these resistors are looking for an audience and followers. They will often prod you for a response, hoping to trip you up and getting you to make a public blunder or obvious error they can exploit. Value them at all times, especially when they are being obnoxious, care for them in their darkest times and their brightest ones. Care for these staff members as well as you do for your best staff members. But, let them know that you are not wavering from the core mission and focus of your school's mission and goals. I must remind you to document everything with this group—keep those e-mails, take notes on conferences with them, and jot down some reflections after meetings with them. I say this because, with this group, I begin to let them know fairly quickly that this behavior will not be tolerated. I ask them if they would accept this behavior from their students, and I remind them that we work in a school that is respectful, responsible, and kind. Lastly, don't reward the overbearing octopus by giving in or giving them what they want. This only serves to feed the monster even more. Instead, hold your ground, build consensus with others, and set your standards high on treatment of one another.

Passive Resistance

Have you ever been taken back by something you observed at a faculty meeting? We have seen some fantastic interaction as well as some behaviors that surprised us. During one meeting, while the principal was talking, two teachers, sitting in the back row, turned their backs on the principal and began to read the newspaper. These two passive resistors regularly resisted any progress by simply ignoring the leader or by doing something off task. They weren't in his face, going crazy shooting off questions, or confronting him on a regular basis. However, these resistors were just as poisonous as any of the others. This type of behavior deteriorates the community and sends a powerful visual of checking out and not buying in to the mission of the school.

This behavior needs to be addressed immediately. We would address this by having an honest, heartfelt, and respectful conversation with them. Again, ask them, "How would you respond if students acted that way in your class?" These passive resistors can build a quick group of followers and begin to spread the dissent quickly, that's why it's important to address this in a caring and respectful manner. I'd begin by keeping good notes on this type of behavior as it demonstrates a clear lack of professionalism and support. Only use these notes if needed. Try your best to win them over with kindness; set clear expectations that reflect your school's mission, goals, and values; and treat them like your best teachers. Go the extra mile for them and show them that they are an important part of the team. This is where team expectations come into play. A common set of expectations for how faculty and staff treat one another can serve as an excellent guide in discussions with these resistors. Consider having your faculty and staff members design and craft a common understanding and expectations for how they will treat one another, how to resolve conflict, and how to behave and participate in meetings.

Hero-building leaders develop a culture and climate that calls those on the fringes to re-engage with the high call of creating the learning our students need for success in school and in life. This is not a coercive or threatening style that wields power haphazardly or makes demands unwisely. Hero leaders create the atmosphere that invites everyone to join the amazing work. The result is much more than compliance, it's commitment.

NEGATIVE SELF-TALK

Leaders often listen to negative self-talk more than any other voice. We talk ourselves into believing lies such as "I'm too young to be a leader," "so many other people are better than me," "I can't deal with conflict," "I need to get out of this job," "my teachers and critics were right about me," "I'll never be successful," or "I can't do this, I'm afraid." These phrases and many more tie us up from truly being free to be successful. I had a young teacher who was constantly rehearsing negative self-talk in his head that he didn't belong in this profession, that he would be better doing his prior job, and he couldn't overcome it. After we talked about negative self-talk and supported him in growing as a teacher, he is now one of our finest teachers.

We all benefit from unwavering support and constant reminders that we can do, or are doing, great things. Be honest and transparent with them, let them know you struggled with negative self-talk at one point in your career. Call them out for the negative self-talk and encourage them to reverse it and infuse positive self-talk into their daily practice. Plus, be sure to provide them the necessary supports to be successful. Lend a helping hand in a class that is unruly, help the teachers make calls home to parents, and let them know you are there every step of the way. This may sound cliché, but positive reinforcement to them is the best way to overcome these resistors. Help them to believe in themselves and see that they are doing great things.

"Most of life's battles are won or lost in the mind."

Craig Groeschel

How do we break the resistance? It's not a matter of pushing back harder. This becomes a battle when what we really desire is a cultural shift. One of the first steps that helps the whole organization move forward together comes in the power of listening—authentically and honestly hearing our resistors and detractors. There can be insightful items that surface in our shared conversations that lead to improved work together. One prompt we both use when focused on listening

> You owe it to yourself to engage your resistors and learn from them.

@DrBillZiegler @DrDaveRamage

is simply, "Tell me more." When resistors feel like they've been listened to and heard—that their ideas, complaints, even rants, have been truly heard—it is a gift we can give as a leader.

If you really believe the leader's voice does not have to be the loudest voice in the room, you owe it to yourself to engage your resistors and learn from them. We also have to realize that sometimes an imposed timeline or other factors prevent us from the luxury of unlimited listening and compromise. But even when a decision has to be made in a timely fashion, we can find time to listen, reflect, and act/adjust accordingly.

Students will have their resistors and detractors, too. We need to model and teach strategies that allow students to find success in their most difficult and frustrating situations. If we create a fantastic culture where students thrive, we are doing a great thing. We also need to equip students with tools and skills that will serve them as they exit the nurturing culture they experience in our schools and enter the competitive environment of adult life. Here are a few key strategies and tools we can give to our students to help them thrive and change their world.

Expand their world by stretching their comfort zone. It's too easy for all of us to simply hang out with people who talk like us, think like us, look like us, read the same books as us, watch the same shows as us, and believe the same things as we do. There is a place for this kind of camaraderie, but we will achieve greater success when we can cross boundaries and bring diverse individuals into a shared mission to work together.

We can also train and empower students by giving them an authentic audience for their work. When the primary person your students are working to persuade or move to action with their idea/solution is their classroom teacher we have failed to give them their best learning environment. We can no longer ignore the flattened world that our communication technology and social media have provided. We need to embrace these tools and cultivate relationships with local businesses and community resources, so our students aren't doing time in school so they can change the world later—they can, and do, change the world now.

HERO SOLUTIONS FOR STUDENTS

Teaching students to overcome the resistors of our world will empower them to thrive in a complex and conflict riddled world. By doing this, we empower them to be leaders not just in our school but our world. The following are some super-power solutions to teach students to win against the resistance they will face:

Unity Day—Several years ago, we partnered with Thom Stecher and Associates to design a Unity Day experience for our school. This is a program where all sixth-grade students are taught about teamwork, conflict resolution, community, legacy, antibullying, accepting others, and overcoming adversity. The Unity Days are still running strong today and are a key part of our middle level schoolwide positive behavior support program. Led by counselors Cristina Kleinfelter and Stephan Kincaid, Unity Day works to bring students together and teach them the skills needed to be successful in our increasingly polarized world. The learning taking place on these special days of training doesn't stop when the school bell sounds—just the opposite. Teachers, administrators, student leaders, and staff work with middle school students to reinforce what was taught during Unity Day. They continue the focus of bringing a community together in all aspects of learning and living together. What started as a one-day event for incoming sixth graders has expanded to every grade level. Much more importantly, Unity Day has grown into a culture of unity and respect. Unity Day helps our Falcon Four tenets come alive: Be Safe, Be Positive, Be Respectful, and Be

Responsible. How can your school come together to teach qualities of respect, acceptance, unity, responsibility, legacy, and conflict resolution?

Most recently, our high school has embraced Josten's Renaissance program, "The Harbor." This series of five-minute videos comes with discussion guides for teachers to lead conversations with the class around character education and social/emotional learning. Students learn about making biased judgments on people, living out their passions, respecting all people, and so much more. Students participate in "The Harbor" twice a month in a pride period class, which includes approximately 20 students in the same grade level. We created expectations for these discussions, asking students to be respectful to others, not talk when others are talking, and to keep the conversation in the room. It's not the time or the place to share what was shared during "The Harbor" time during lunch or while hanging out with friends. Our goal is twofold, lead our school in simultaneously learning about character and social emotional learning and build smaller learning communities in our school where friendships are built, connections are made, and trust is nurtured. In addition, the Jostens Renaissance program has transformed our school community into one of celebration and a focus on all kids. Our positive principal referrals strengthen our ability to celebrate kids, and our staffulty celebrations celebrate the work of our staffulty (staff and faculty combined). These celebrations have ignited a culture of appreciation, value, and recognition that builds capacity and strengthens relationships. We even partnered with the local Chick-Fil-A to recognize four students a month who are our Chick-Fil-A champions. The owner and operator of our local Chick-Fil-A comes to our school, and sometimes he even brings the Chick-Fil-A cow mascot with him, as we celebrate together the achievements of our students. Each student receives a certificate, a CFA free sandwich coupon, a drawstring backpack, and is featured on our social media. Recognitions like these give us an opportunity to celebrate and recognize the real heroes in our schools, and it builds a hero-building school culture that thrives.

Conflict Management—In the hero world, conflict is everywhere and around every turn. Whether it's the road rage of a reckless driver, the unruly fans clashing with one another at a local game, or the rant between two people that never ends on social media, conflict is part of our world. We need to teach kids how to resolve conflict in responsible and respectful ways that will help them thrive in our complex world. Here are some hero solutions that will help any students be ready to resolve the conflict that comes their way:

Not responding. Not everything requires a response. Sometimes it's best to pause, wait, step back, and refrain from responding. Not responding does not mean doing nothing. The first decision is to resist a knee-jerk reaction, but the real work is in the wise consideration of the choice to not respond.

Hero Sounding Board. Find a trusted hero person that you can get feedback from and guidance on next steps. Even though we suggested not responding all of the time, there are times when you need to engage, and waiting, or pretending the problem will go away on its own, can serve to increase the severity of the problem. Sometimes we do need to act and to act prudently. Just like the reckless road rage driver, emotions can drive our actions and decision making. Reinforce with students the importance of making decisions and resolving conflict outside of intense emotions. When anger, jealousy, or hatred come into play, everyone loses out. I know this can be hard, but encourage them to stick to the facts and use "I" statements such as "I feel frustrated when you . . " or, "I was hurt when you said . . ." We can help kids work on these skills by modeling and teaching them. It is our responsibility as leaders to make sure that students are learning these skills.

A great way to teach these skills is in the world of school discipline. We need to stop jumping to the punitive consequences and use acting out or poor behavior as an opportunity to teach a proper response. Talking with students about how the victim might have felt builds empathy, a skill much needed in our world today. Or, talking about how they could have handled the situation differently allows students to reflect and learn from their mistakes.

When I was an assistant principal, our school resource officer led a program called peer mediation. The SRO worked with a group of students to get trained in how to resolve conflicts with their peers. When a conflict would arise in the school, the SRO would have the peer mediation student leaders work with the students to resolve the matter. This provided students with authentic opportunities to resolve conflict and to contribute positively to their school.

Empowering Leaders—Work as hard as possible to provide leadership opportunities for students in your school. Whether it's the class leader leading her classmates to lunch or recess, the co-captain leading his team, or the section leader in band, find ways to empower students to be leaders. Even in small ways this can be done in the classroom. Assign students various roles and responsibilities in the class, teach students how to present the morning announcements, or develop a team to return the cafeteria to regular status after each lunch. Too often in schools, we keep using the same students to lead. Intentionally search for ways to include more students in leadership, and rotate out the leadership positions so everyone can experience the responsibility of leadership. These leadership roles are perfect opportunities to teach students how to overcome the resistors and how to prepare in a way that reduces the resistance from the start. Once you develop leaders, use the older students as key leaders to teach the younger students the qualities of leadership that the school expects.

Empowering leaders creates a need to develop and foster leaders. This is best done by providing a mentorship program for older, more mature students to mentor younger students in leadership roles. By doing this, you quickly multiply your reach and expand your audience of leaders. It's vital that students see and follow student leaders who reflect their demographics. We need to be intentional in developing leaders from all groups in our schools. Leaders should be selected and nurtured from all ethnic backgrounds, religions, sexual orientations, ages, genders, socioeconomic levels, and ability levels.

The Power of a Story—Whenever we hear someone tell a story, we are immediately drawn in to listen and be attentive. We instantly look to make practical and personal connections to the story and to see what we can learn from the story. We believe strongly in the power of a story. Use the stories of your older students and how they learned from their experience, how they overcame the resistors, how they grew as leaders, and what they are doing now. These stories can motivate even the most reluctant learner and empower them into leadership in a way you never imagined. Take time to journal and archive these stories through video and podcasting. This way, students can look back on students that attended the school and the difference they are making in the district or community later in life. By taking the time to document and archive these stories, you provide a library of resources for anyone in the school to draw from and to use to inspire students. The power of a story captured on video or audio can go a long way in motivating students. Maybe use one of the best clips as a part of your school's orientation for new students, as a midyear motivator shown to the entire school, or as a social media campaign on overcoming adversity.

Leverage social media to tell the stories of students and how they overcame resistors and adversity. Use social media tools to get these stories out to the public but also as a way to encourage others to tell their stories. Share your own personal story of how you overcame resistors, as the power of a story cannot be understated. A good story that can be supported with pictures and video can move and inspire students to overcome their resistors and thrive in life. Ask your teachers to take one day to share a personal story of overcoming adversity in their life with students. During March Madness, our school focuses on preparing and bringing attention to colleges and universities. We ask teachers to take a few minutes each day to share their personal stories about how they chose their colleges, the greatest challenges they faced in college and how they overcame them, how they accessed resources while at school, and how they got connected on campus. We ask them to relay these messages through the power of a story.

Most elementary schools celebrate the 100th day of school, and we encourage you to put a new twist or addition on your 100th day of school celebrations. Be intentional in weaving a story into this day by having teachers share a story where they gave, or didn't give, 100 percent to a project, activity, or event, and share how it worked out. Have the teachers draw pictures on the board showing their efforts. Everyone has a story, we need to unravel those stories and share them out with students. From your custodian, administrative assistants, counselors, principals, teachers, and volunteers, take one day, and ask them to share their story with students—a story of overcoming a resistor, a story of building a relationship, or a story about how they fulfilled a dream.

HERO SIGHTING

"Knowing that experts forget how hard it was for them to learn, we can understand the need to look at the learning process through students' eyes, rather than making presumptions about how students 'should be' learning" (Hattie & Yates, 2014. p.12).

Reflect with your team. How are you gathering—and listening to—student voice in your school? Have you recently experienced some new learning that caused you to begin as a novice? What new experience would help you gain that kind of perspective—new language? New musical instrument? Coding? Painting?

This is a reminder for us to step back and make sure we recognize the abundance of opportunities our students (and beginning teachers) encounter that invite persistence. Especially if you are a seasoned veteran, take time to step away, reflect, and acknowledge that outright failure is probably not the only condition that points to a need for resilience. Ask your students, peers, or leadership team how the learning is going and where there's a need to encourage one another over a stubborn spot or difficult aspect of the work. We all need to build resilience in our learning practices and our collective culture.

HERO TRAINING

Use these activities to nurture your skills. Even better—gather with your team to embed these skills in your work and empower your students to become heroes that change their world.

1. Hero SIM—Work with your leadership team to complete this 6.0 Hero SIM on Beating the Resistance!!

WHADITW Reflection Questions

2. What is your WHADITW moment, and how have you overcome it?
3. How is your WHADITW holding you and your school back from moving forward?
4. What can you and your team do to move beyond WHADITW toward progress and growth for kids?
5. To help get a sense of where the greatest resistance is coming from, consider doing the Shadow A Student challenge from Stanford University's dSchool. Encourage several members of your leadership team to participate. Find out more about Shadow A Student and the dSchool at https://dschool.stanford.edu/shadow-a-student-k12.
6. The Power of a Story—Share your learning or leadership story with someone on your team or with a student.
7. List three resistors in your school in the space below, and outline what you are going to do to beat the resistance.

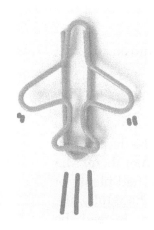

GO BIG OR GO HOME

Empower Students to Be Global Game Changers!

"The leadership instinct you are born with is the backbone. You develop the funny bone and the wishbone that go with it."

—Elaine Agather

SHOES FOR ESPERANZA

You've probably had students approach you with "a great idea" or "simple question" they wanted to share about changes at school—and honoring student voice can be a powerful culture builder. Hero-building leaders know the best ideas come from the whole group, not just their own thinking and planning. This next story started with that kind of interaction. One day, on her way to board her bus, a student asked her principal, "Can we collect shoes for kids who don't have any?" That simple request turned into one the most far-reaching impacts we've experienced as school leaders.

Over the ensuing months, that question grew into an amazing project called Shoes for Esperanza.

The question came during one of the first days of school. Earlier that summer, Mia had the opportunity to visit Guatemala with her family. While she was there, she developed an awareness of the poverty in that country and the detrimental effects it had on the children and adults she met there. Mia also realized that she, like many of her peers, had plenty of shoes in her closet that she no longer wore. Thankfully, the principal didn't ignore that simple question. Instead, he took some steps to engage Mia for more details. He also connected Mia with a teacher who had experience assisting students with community service projects. This turned a small group of students, and their teacher/sponsor, into a force for change.

Soon, the entire school was involved in a shoe drive. The goal was to collect enough shoes to help some children and package them in a container that would head to Guatemala. Students, and their parents, were enthusiastic in their efforts, and pairs of shoes started showing up in homeroom collection boxes—sneakers, sandals, boots, heels, flats, Uggs, dress shoes, slippers, moccasins, sliders, work boots, all kinds of footwear! What started as a simple question resulted in thousands of donated shoes. Shoes for Esperanza gathered so many shoes that an alternate project was needed to raise the funds to ship them!

By the time the school year ended, we had collected enough shoes to supply a local charity with winter boots (not a great need for the families in Guatemala) and six communities in Guatemala with hope, encouragement, and shoes. A local church agreed to receive the containers and act as a central location to distribute shoes. Mia and her family returned to Guatemala to hand out the footwear to children and their parents. Shoes for Esperanza was an example of what it means to "go big." It not only collected more shoes than we ever expected, it created hope, hope for local students who wondered if their lives would mean anything to their community or their world and hope for families in an impoverished country that wondered if their lives were seen as valuable at all.

Mia is an authentic global game changer. Her thoughtfulness, empathy, and idea were great. But most importantly, her action to do something about the problem resulted in a tremendous lesson for our students and an amazing blessing for families in Guatemala. Never underestimate what the power of a heartfelt request may grow to produce. Provide the resources and leadership that allows students to change the world now. Don't make them wait until they grow up to do this work.

GIVE a HAND

Our next global game changer, Gabriel Fillippini, a junior at Park View in Loudoun County, Virginia, was focused on changing his brother's life for the better. Gabriel's brother, six-year-old Lucas, was born without a left hand. Gabriel decided to ask his teacher to use the school's technology to make his brother a hand. Park View teacher Kurt O'Connor had no experience in building prosthetic hands, but he didn't let that stop him. Gabriel and Mr. O'Connor used the school's 3-D printer to print out Lucas's hand. They collaborated with key community members to find resources and assistance in perfecting the prosthetic. It took multiple tries, prototypes, and attempts to perfect the hand that would fit Lucas's arm and work like an actual hand. Gabriel was passionate about this project because it directly impacted his little brother's life.

> A Virginia high school student's bold request to use the school's 3-D printer soon became a life-changing milestone for his little brother in need of a prosthetic hand. Gabriel Fillippini, a junior at Park View High School in Loudoun County, Virginia, was inspired to help his 6-year-old brother, Lucas, who was born with no left hand, as soon as he discovered the school had obtained a 3-D printer for its career and technical

education classroom. On his 6th birthday, earlier this month, Lucas received an unforgettable present—a new hand that fit him perfectly. "It's nice to do things with my both hands," Lucas said, adding that he is grateful that kids can no longer ask about his "little hand." (Carey & Hartleb, 2016)

Park View High School Principal Kirk Dolson shared with me how it's important for school leaders to build a culture of exploration and creativity. "It begins when we model innovation and solving real-world problems that will improve the lives of others." He went on to share how many of his teachers are doing amazing things with students to solve real world problems. Kirk, and his team of teachers and staff, have turned around Park View high school to help students find success. The prosthetic hand could not have been created if it wasn't for the leadership of his brother's teacher, Mr. O'Connor and the culture that his principal created. "Our culture is all about transparency, you have to be open to criticism, ingenuity, and different ways of doing things. We are a collaborative culture, students are working together to solve today's real world problems" (Ziegler, 2018).

Gabriel is a global game changer because he saw a problem, worked creatively and collaboratively to fix it, and improved the quality of life for his brother. He didn't use the 3-D printer to create a drone or a game piece. Instead, he used technology to transform his brother's life by building him a hand that would radically change his life.

Kangaroo Cup

Lily Born saw that her grandfather was knocking over his cup every time he went to take a drink. Lily's grandfather had Parkinson's disease and struggled to hold a regular cup. This bothered Lily and inspired her to kick into action. At the age of seven, Lily worked with her father to create a cup that her grandfather would be able to use. She invented the Kangaroo Cup, a three-legged cup that didn't spill over. Lily's invention rose in popularity and had her presenting at the White House, and her story was told on *NBC Nightly News*, *CNN Headline News*, *NPR Weekend Edition*, and several local news affiliates. But most importantly, it allowed her grandfather to take a drink without spilling his cup on the floor, requiring it to be cleaned up. Here's a short segment from Lily's website:

> Using moldable plastic and a bit of experimenta-
> tion, she made him a plastic cup that didn't tip and
> was comfortable. About a year later, she noticed her
> dad trying to save his laptop from spilled coffee, and
> she made him a ceramic version at a local pottery
> studio. After using it for a short time, and realizing
> what a great invention it was, Lily's dad asked her if
> she wanted to bring it into production. That began
> an adventure that had them up to elbows in clay and
> traveling across the world to the ceramics capital of
> China, JingDeZhen. There they were able to refine the
> models, find a manufacturer and prepare for a pro-
> duction run of ceramic cups. Thanks to supporters on
> Kickstarter and Indiegogo, the ceramic Kangaroo Cup
> became a reality. Lily continues to be a role model for
> kids everywhere and an inspiration to makers of all
> ages. (Imagiroo, 2018)

SADDLE INNOVATION

Three global game changers in our school are students who are working to create a saddle accessory that makes it easier for students with special needs to ride horses. These students appreciate how equine therapy can play an important part in a child's recovery and progress, but they also know that rid-ing a horse can be difficult. That's why three students from our school designed a pad to place beneath a horse saddle that has light-emitting diode (LED) light bars on it to show riders where they need to lean to balance on the center of the saddle. Last year at our school's Shark Tank program, this team won the top prize to continue to hone their saddle and to work toward a patent. Much like Mia, Hannah, Gabe, and Lily, these students identified a problem and worked to fix the problem to improve the quality of life for someone or a group of people. These global game changers are continuing to work to design this saddle so students with special needs can ride horses and enjoy riding just like anyone else. These students saw a need for students with physical or mental impairments participating in equine therapy. They went on to design and build a saddle component that gave immediate, visual feedback to riders that increased their ability to balance dynamically and improved their riding success.

Rain Garden

An environmental class at our high school identified a problem with drainage after renovations and a redesign of our front parking lot. Rainwater was running off of the parking lot and gathering in a swamp-like pit at the end of the parking lot. The students and their teacher, Mr. Adams, worked together and partnered with 3M, a company in the suburbs of Philadelphia, along with other groups, to locate funding and create a rain garden in the swampy area. They did the planning, researched plants that would be good to use, and found funding for their project. They sought approval from the district and worked to install the rain garden for our community to enjoy. This class identified a real problem in our district and worked to turn it into rain garden that our community is proud of. The students aren't stopping with this rain garden, they are currently working to beautify our courtyard and to design another rain garden on campus. Thanks to the leadership of Mr. Adams and his students, our school now has a rain garden to recycle rain runoff into a rain garden that improves the environmental impact of our school campus.

OCEAN CLEANUP

Our next global game changers are a school of middle-level students working to clean up our oceans of plastic waste. Harrisburg Middle School students, under the leadership of Principal Darren Ellwein, are working collaboratively with students in Norway to remove plastic water bottles and other plastic trash from the ocean. They are going to Costa Rica this summer to serve on an international council and join other global game changers doing similar work.

Harrisburg middle schoolers are coming up with innovative ideas to stop or reduce ocean pollution. Twenty-eight billion pounds of plastic end up in the ocean every year. Their three-week project is forcing them to think creatively and to connect with business professionals around the world. They're being asked to come up with prototypes that could help rid the ocean of harmful plastics. Sixth grader Hannah Pierson is having a blast. She shares, "It's a like a fish tank filter, but it's going to be a lot bigger." At the end of the period, students are recording what they built into an app that can be viewed around the world. "I love doing this. It makes my mind work more. I think it's a lot better way of learning," Pierson said (Holsen, 2017).

Harrisburg Principal Darren Ellwein shares,

> Our students are working to solve problems that directly affect our world, they are given an open time during the day to research, investigate, and brainstorm how to clean up our oceans. The best part is that they are not doing this alone, they are partnering with a school in Norway and with students from around the world to make our oceans cleaner.

All global game changers have something in common: they see a problem and they work to fix it. It doesn't matter if the solution supports one person, a group of patients with the same condition, an entire community, or the world. If the student positively impacts one person and improves his or her quality of life, the student becomes part of the worldwide assembly of students changing the world, a.k.a., global game changers.

We like to use this acronym to challenge our thinking with "Go Big"!

G—Go After a Problem: Students see a problem in our world, whether it's providing shoes for kids who don't have them, creating a prosthetic hand for his brother, designing a nonspillable cup for her grandfather, or trying to clean the ocean of plastics, they go after the problem and tirelessly work to solve the problem. They innovate, collaborate, communicate, and calculate how to solve the problem.

O—Others Focused: Global game changers realize that life isn't just about them. They work to improve the lives of others. They don't innovate for fun or entertainment; they innovate to change lives for the better. They remember that a king fights for his kingdom, but a hero fights for everyone.

B—Believe: Students believe that they can change the world, they are tirelessly committed to solving real-life problems, and they believe in themselves and their team to find a solution to the problem.

I—Interested: These global game changers are passionate about their work, they are highly interested in the project, and they can't stop thinking about it and working on it. Sometimes, the project consumes them as they seek to find a solution to the problem. Regardless, the project is something that highly piques the interest of the students involved.

G—Global Mindset: These students see beyond their own world. They understand the importance of having a global mindset that works to improve their world. And, they diligently work to make their world a better place, one that is enriched by their contributions to society.

How are you helping students gain a global mindset? Use the ideas and stories we've shared to inspire your work to empower students toward a global mindset with learning and leading. By doing this, we teach students to focus on others, to

Figure 7.1   GO BIG Reflection

How is your school doing on preparing students to do the following:	Not Even Close	Stumbling Forward	Making Progress— Not There Yet	Going Big— Hitting It Out of the Ballpark
Go After a Problem				
Be Others-Focused				
Believe				
Get Interested				
Have a Global Mindset				

look beyond their own circumstances, and to seek solutions to complex problems to help others.

THINK BIG, ACT BIG

[Dave] At this point in my career I had already spent 11 years in the classroom and was working in my second year as an instructional coach for all our schools. I got a message that Art Tinner, our superintendent, wanted to see me, and I immediately wondered what I had done wrong. Isn't it amazing how we always assume the worst? When I arrived at his office and we had a chance to talk together, the conversation quickly centered on the instructional coaching I was doing for our schools. He asked me if I planned to get a principal certification to gain an increased leadership role in our school district. In my idealism, I talked about the multiple reasons why I could make a bigger impact by changing one classroom at a time. I had started some really strong initiatives with our professional staff, and the coaching experience was challenging and professionally fulfilling. Computers were beginning to show up more frequently in schools, and I was all about this new way to teach and learn. When he asked about a bigger impact, I wrote him off because I knew the kind of impact I could have by leading with coaching and technology integration.

My optimism (or naiveté) continued into my doctoral studies, in fact, it influenced my choice of doctoral program. I resisted the traditional programs that existed in several excellent universities nearby. The program at Drexel stood out because it connected the School of Education (SoE) with other disciplines like engineering, computer science, and design. Because of Drexel's strong leadership focus I actually had credentials to be a superintendent—and still no principal certification. What I failed to see during that conversation with Art many years ago was his desire to get me to "go bigger." I was thinking big, but I wasn't really acting big. Idealism has its place, but in reality, I wasn't taking a very efficient path toward the systemwide change I was trying to influence. My desire for impact was strong, but I wasn't taking the Go Big kinds of steps I really needed to accomplish the vision. Don't misunderstand me, the coursework and research during my PhD work was some of the best learning I have ever experienced. It was "going big" in a different way than Art was suggesting.

Guess what I did about a year after I attained my PhD? I got my principal certification. I've been in education for more than 30 years, and I've enjoyed a variety of roles and experiences. Nothing has been more energizing than serving a single school in the daily work of learning and leading. If you are considering a next step in school leadership, I would echo remnants of my conversation with Art Tinner and tell you to Go Big!

One thing that we love about heroes is that they never seem to do things small. Heroes go big or go home because they understand the condition and survival of the world

depends on them and their success. Instead of being paralyzed by fear, they work through doubts and opposition to
keep the big goal in mind. The reality is that even these huge
goals are accomplished with purposeful, incremental steps.
You may have to change your view.

EXPAND YOUR VIEW

Go Big or Go Home learning requires educators to have a new
VIEW on learning. The acronym of VIEW stands for Value,
Innovation, Empower, and World. This new VIEW requires
educators to shift their thinking and to have the courage and
desire to shatter the status quo. It requires us to examine what
we value as educators, to innovate for real and sustainable
change, and to empower students to be world-focused global
game changers. We can no longer focus on our own myopic
view of life; we must take the whole world into our lens as we
educate our next generation of students. We can expand our
VIEW to transform our cultures of learning and create out of
this world learning for every student. Consider the VIEW areas.

Is the work you're creating for students Valuable? Who is
it valuable for? Does it begin and end with your chapter, unit,
and assessment, or does it make a substantive difference for
someone beyond your classroom walls?

We've spoken about Innovation in earlier chapters, but
it's worth considering each time you begin to design learning
for your students. Are you falling into old habits, or are you
seeking fresh solutions and approaches to learning goals and
processes?

Does the work you're asking students and teachers to do
actually Empower them? Are you willing to give away control and power to enable more authentic empowerment in the
small, and big, details of the task?

How big is your focus? Can you see a new World out
there? Does the learning move beyond the classroom walls?
Are others coming into the school to expand your worldview?

Figure 7.2 VIEW Finder

VIEW Finder	Where Our Focus Has Been	Where Our Focus Will Shift	Examples of Ways Your School Represents Each of These Global Game-Changing Qualities
Value			
Innovation			
Empower			
World			

Now that you've thought about your VIEW, use the reflection tool in Figure 7.2 to work with your team and check your vision. Use the VIEW Finder to plan areas you may want to focus on in the near future.

The idea of changing the world can be overwhelming. Be encouraged that Going Big can begin by starting small. Let's get beyond the classroom walls and make a change for a whole academic team, grade level, school, district, and community. In our own schools, we have seen students tackle problems that resulted in some amazing results. One group addressed a problem following on-site renovations by designing and installing a rain garden. Another group of senior high students chose community heroes—police officers, firefighters, EMTs, or other first responders—and they contacted them to collect their pictures to create portraits of these local heroes that will eventually be published in a book along with additional text that we can distribute electronically to our students and community. Yet another group of young middle school programmers worked with elementary school teachers to design and code a game experience to help emerging readers learn their sight words. All these examples show that students can change the world for themselves, their peers, their community, and beyond.

Is learning worth learning if it doesn't result in making a difference in our world? By observing that, "education is the most powerful weapon which you can use to change the world," Nelson Mandela challenges us to leverage education to make a difference in our world. As leaders, our actions have a direct impact on this change. If we neglect our duty as leaders of pushing others to make an authentic difference in the lives of others, we risk creating learning that reaches a dead end very quickly. It's good for the next in-class assessment, and that's about it. But when learning results in making a difference in our world, the quality of learning is improved—and quality of life also improves! We regularly teach learning that has zero impact on our world, for example, making kids memorize the state capitals, having kids play Kahoot!™ games, or having them recall facts for assignments that begin and end in the classroom.

The ability for students and teachers to be global game changers is directly related to the culture that the leader creates and nurtures in the school community. When leaders nurture a culture of innovation, problem solving, and authentic learning, global game changers are set loose to change our world for the better.

LEADING BIG

One way to Go Big is to find that singular event or focus that will catapult you to a global project or phenomenon. The more likely way you will lead your students and staff to big opportunities is to grow the beliefs and plans to embed within your learning culture. Mitch Resnick of the MIT Media Lab talks about this kind of culture when he implores, "Today everyone needs to be a risk-taker, a doer, a maker of things—not necessarily to bend the arc of history, but to bend the arcs of their own lives" (2017, p. 32). To create this type of culture, leaders should pay attention to some global game-changing factors that can transform your culture and your leadership. Here are nine to consider:

Learning Culture—Focus on learning, be a voracious learner who is constantly growing and developing as a leader. Even more, build a culture where everyone is a learner. For example, our librarian placed signs on everyone's doors that say, "I'm reading . . ." and you have to fill in what you are reading. I wonder what it would look like if we changed these signs to read, "I'm learning . . . ". Hopefully your sign would change frequently. Plus, learning doesn't always have to be about school, but school always needs to be about learning. You can talk about how you are learning about fly fishing, gardening, home renovation, bass playing, cooking, drawing, and so on; the list is endless.

> Focus on learning, be a voracious learner who is constantly growing and developing as a leader, and build a culture where everyone is a learner.
>
> @DrBillZiegler @DrDaveRamage

Galactic Learning—One thing that makes so many heroes rockin' awesome is that they travel between galaxies. Star-Lord, from Guardians of the Galaxies, was born on earth but then ended up traveling all over the galaxy and beyond. It's time to tear down the walls and open the doors of learning. Leverage the resources in your community and region to deepen student learning opportunities. Look for ways to expand opportunities for your students beyond your school's campus. We like to say, "School has left the building."

Learning Connections—Students need to make connections to others in their learning. Learning in isolation loses traction. It's difficult to get feedback to improve and to overcome obstacles, and it can run off the tracks if connections don't provide the guidance needed. Creativity in problem solving also requires connections. It takes connections to the ideas of others, and it takes connections to other perspectives and disciplines to gain the best solutions.

Agile Learning—Students must adapt and change to remain relevant in our fast-paced world. Our world is changing and accelerating at an alarming rate, and our learning needs to keep up. Our learning needs to be agile. Our systems of public education are particularly slow to change, but if we are going to become relevant again, we need to continually change and re-invent the way we teach and learn.

Authentic Skills—Learning needs to be so much more than pencil and paper, it needs to provide students with authentic learning experiences that empower them to grow and develop in complex situations. It's time we give up our multiple-choice problems and have students dig in and learn how to solve today's complex problems. Hypothetical situations in a word problem can no longer be the gold standard for authenticity. We are living in a world that allows connectivity and collaboration to all corners of the planet. When we ask students to display their mastery of a skill/concept or to demonstrate their understanding of a key aspect of our curriculum, the teacher can no longer be the sole audience, expert, and evaluator. Push learning into the world to gain authentic skills for your students.

Digital Power—It's time to stop having kids power down and instead have them power up to learn. When students use digital resources to research, design, create, communicate, resolve, publish, and evaluate, they are ready to tackle the myriad of challenges that come their way. Alan November discusses a digital shift he learned about from his daughter in 1998 that still impacts his work today. He relates how www.fanfiction.net allowed his daughter, and others, to gain an audience that was much larger than their teacher or classmates. In this specific case, students were extending the stories of Harry Potter while J. K. Rowling was working on the next book in the series. The slow pace of publishing created a demand for new stories. One particular student author came to November's attention, and when he asked why she was writing so well but not completing her class assignments she replied, "Every day when I wake up, I have an important decision to make. Do I write for my teacher or publish to the world? I prefer to publish to the world" (November, 2017).

Hero Failing—Create a culture that allows students, faculty, and staff the freedom to fail. Encourage risk taking, model overcoming failure, and talk about how we learn from failure. Each new iteration and design includes testing that confirms success or indicates where redesign is needed. Learning is the same. Each time we fail as leaders, or learners, we have the chance to look closely, redesign, implement the new changes, and try again. This iterative approach is exactly what world-class engineers and designers incorporate into their daily work. Schools should, too.

Storytelling—We have chosen to weave stories throughout this book to help us all learn and lead. The power of storytelling can't be underestimated in learning. Tell your school's story through social media, share stories of student success, and showcase how your school is inspiring students on a regular basis. The most popular posts on our social media sites are the ones that feature students, faculty, and staff members. By celebrating their work and telling the story of their successes, everyone grows. Stories also reinforce the cultural beliefs that will bring a change in the purpose and mission of your school. Do you want to be more global? Tell stories of your teachers and students that are connecting beyond your classroom.

Windows and Mirrors—Looking through big, panoramic windows can really inspire you, and describing that picture may help others follow you to new, expanded vistas for your school to engage with. But it's vital that we also take time for a good look in the mirror. By taking time to reflect, we evaluate our ability to move forward. Journal, blog, or podcast to reflect on your growth. Create a team that reflects on learning. More importantly, encourage teachers to use reflection in their daily practices with students.

HERO SIGHTING

In one recent Canadian study, 4- to 6-year-old children participated in a 20-day computerised (sic) program for music listening, pitch, and melody. Compared to others, these students showed significant gains on two intellectual tests, a vocabulary test, and a measure of inhibitory control. (Hattie & Yates, 2014 p. 209)

Reflect with your team. How do your schedule, curriculum, and focus reflect a value for arts and creativity? What are some steps you can take to ensure every student has a chance to create?

We include this example from Hattie's work to remind all of us that breaking the status quo can be an important way we choose to Go Big! Instead of eliminating what some call "extraneous learning," consider ways to change, enhance, and expand your entire approach. When you Go Big, remember to give it time, and include an evaluation component to help determine how your changes are producing (or failing to produce) the results you are looking for. Plan with your leadership team, and plan your next step to find a way to Go Bigger than you are right now.

HERO TRAINING

Use these activities to nurture your skills. Even better—gather with your team to embed these skills in your work and empower your students to become heroes that change their world.

1. To find out how to design and lead learning to create global game changers, look into challenge-based learning at https://cbl.digitalpromise.org.
2. Share your global game-changer stories with us, and others, through social media. Work with your team to create a short video clip or blog post, and consider including student voices to show the way your leadership work is impacting students and families.
3. Use #HBLschools on Twitter to share how your students are doing amazing things to make our world a better place.
4. Reflect on and complete Figures 7.1 GO BIG Reflection and 7.2 VIEW Finder.

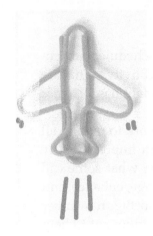

BE COURAGEOUS
Risk It All for What's Right

"I learned that courage was not the absence of fear, but the triumph over it. The brave man is not he who does not feel afraid, but he who conquers that fear."

—Nelson Mandela

ORIGIN STORIES

Most heroes have an origin story that helps define their calling and purpose. Whose leadership story are you playing a part in as a mentor or an encourager? What's your leadership origin story? How does your story define your leadership? Maybe you've never really considered these questions, but your story impacts your leadership style, goals, approach, and much more. Our origin and leadership stories continue to influence and inform our leadership journey.

[Dave] I was only the second person in my immediate or extended family to graduate from college. My two younger brothers followed that path and became college graduates as well. I would have been the very first in our family, but my mom beat me by about 10 years. You may be struggling with the math here. My mom returned to finish a teaching degree when I was in middle school, but the story begins long before that heroic feat. Education was always valued in my house, and reading was a normal part of our daily routines. Some of my earliest memories at home include being read to as a child. Growing up in the coal region of north central Pennsylvania did not carry an expectation of academic pursuit. This was a hard-working, blue collar area, and manual labor was highly valued. I was influenced by strong role models but also heard the cultural voices that did not necessarily place a high value on pursuing a career as a teacher—especially a music teacher. Some of my high school teachers questioned how I could have success in math and science yet intend to pursue a music degree. (I have no doubt they were well-meaning and wished for my success, they just couldn't envision it in music teaching.)

Others were true naysayers: "You'll never be able to afford college," "You'll waste your real talents being a music teacher," or "Stick around and work here like the rest of us," but I was determined to pursue a degree. I was also encouraged by my parents to look beyond my small town, family history of education, or any other limits that were perceived as obstacles. In essence, my parents encouraged me to Go Big!

By the way, my mom not only completed that initial BS degree, she went on to earn a master's degree as a reading specialist and influenced many lives as a junior and senior high social studies teacher and reading specialist. I also broke through the limits of a traditional coal cracker and earned my BS, MEd, and PhD. I've been blessed to serve as a middle school teacher, instructional coach, middle school principal, and district office director. I know that sharing my origin story with some of the students and staff I've met over my career has encouraged them to break through barriers and Go Big, too. I want my own origin story to remind me of the calling, purpose, and responsibilities of leading. I also want my story to serve as a catalyst in the origin story of leaders who will follow me and take up this same calling of hero-building leadership in our schools.

SUPER COURAGEOUS FORTITUDE

When I "Bill" go to new doctors, they frequently ask me, "What do you do for a living?" I proudly respond, "I'm a principal!" I get the same response almost every time: "I would never want to do that, that's a tough job." I usually just smile and tell them how much I love my job and how I have the best job in the world. I find it interesting that doctors, who deal with life and death on a daily basis, find our job as school leaders so difficult. The doctors often go on to share experiences they have had with their school principals growing up. Being a school leader is one of the most challenging professions in the world. Every day, we lead the safety, learning, and culture of hundreds, or thousands, of students in our school. This takes immeasurable courage. Leading with courage empowers our staff and students to do amazing things.

We saved courage for the last hero trait because we believe all of our other hero-building work stems from this one. If we don't have the courage to see through the invisible backpacks kids bring to school, detect truths, debunk myths, listen to student voice, lead like an alien, beat the resistance, and go big or go home, we will never be great leaders—leaders who provide sustainable transformation that truly empowers students.

Being a leader in education is more challenging than ever. Today's schools and districts need leaders who are committed and focused on learning, leading, and building culture. If we can build powerful learning opportunities that make connections, build relevancy, and challenge thinking, students will thrive in our complex world. And, if we can teach, model, and lead in a way that develops leaders, our students will be empowered to overcome insurmountable odds to fulfill their dreams. We all know without a great and positive school culture no organization can move forward with sustainability. We must build a caring, courageous culture together.

Cathy Lassiter's work around courage for school leaders is refreshingly inspiring as she focuses on the need for moral courage. In her book, *Everyday Courage for School Leaders*, she shares,

> Moral courage is the courage to stand up for one's beliefs in the face of overwhelming opposition. It is a synonym for civil courage. Those with moral courage stand up and speak out when injustices occur, human rights are violated, or when persons are treated unfairly. Moral courage is the outward expression of the leader's personal values and core beliefs, and the resulting actions are focused on a greater good. (Lassiter, 2017, p. 13)

Courage is a hero skill that we can learn. In the following sections, you'll see some strategies to develop courage that will transform learning, leadership, and culture. It's also a skill that students need to learn and embrace if they are going to be successful in our complex world. When students have courage, they have a skill that will help them overcome the challenges of life and thrive in their world.

COURAGE TO BE AUTHENTIC

If you watch any hero movie, you will find a hero who doubts his or her ability, tries to mimic what other heroes are doing, or fights the mental struggle of accepting who he or she is. Some have walked away from their superpower or even abandoned it at the cost of others. Even heroes struggle with the courage to be authentic.

Sadly, too many of us lead in a way that doesn't reflect who we truly are or what we represent. This reminds me of when I was a student at college learning to be a teacher. The professor, teaching about classroom management, stressed the importance of not smiling until Thanksgiving. He said the students needed to see you as serious and meaning business. Personally, I thought the professor was crazy, and I knew there was no way that I could do that. However, as a young substitute teacher, I decided to listen to the sage wisdom of this professor. Wow, that just wasn't me! I can't go very long without smiling. That's just who I am, and there's nothing wrong with that. I'm so glad that I put that professor's teachings aside and embraced who I was as a person and a teacher.

As a young school leader, I found myself mirroring what I saw in other leaders rather than being myself. I wanted to be like other leaders that I observed and knew. Sadly, I quickly discovered what I learned in my school leadership courses missed the mark in preparing me for the challenges of the job.

> Students and staff don't need you to be perfect, they need you to be authentic.
>
> @DrBillZiegler @DrDaveRamage

What we learned, through our years of school leadership, is that your students and staff don't need you to be perfect, they need you to be authentic. We need to stop striving for perfection, stop seeking popularity, stop searching for approval, stop working to please others, and stop listening to our naysayers. Instead, we need to be empowered to be authentic. Being authentic means we are real. Being real in front of our faculty, staff, students, parents, and community builds trust and a reputation as someone who truly cares about students. Be upfront and honest about your mistakes. Be transparent and upfront about your shortcomings. Say you are sorry—admit mistakes. Share your passions, vision, and focus. Be you, and let your personality shine through your leadership. Have fun. Smile! As one successful leader reminds us:

> Your time is limited, so don't waste it living someone else's life. Don't be trapped by dogma—which is living with the results of other people's thinking. Don't let the noise of others' opinions drown out your own inner voice. And most important, have the courage to follow your heart and intuition.
>
> Steve Jobs

Table 8.1   Authentic Reflection Tool

	I Need to Grow in This Area	I'm Doing Alright	I GOT THIS!!!
Be upfront and honest about your mistakes.			
Be transparent and upfront about your shortcomings.			
Say you are sorry— admit your mistakes.			
Share your passions, vision, and focus.			
Be you, let your personality shine through your leadership.			
Have fun.			
Smile.			

Focus on the areas you scored high on in Table 8.1, and use them to strengthen your hero-building culture. In the areas you need to develop, work to collaborate with others, add more leadership tools to your skillset, and network with other school leaders to strengthen these areas in order to nurture an authentic learning culture in your school.

COURAGE TO ASK FOR HELP

Asking for help is not the superpower of many heroes. They often struggle alone until their partner or someone intervenes and forces them to reach out and ask for help. Whether it is Superman asking Lois Lane for guidance, Iron Man asking Pepper for help, or Wonder Woman asking Queen Hippolyta for direction, heroes eventually realize that they are stronger when they are asking for help and guidance.

I would bet that you don't like to ask for help. I know I don't. I'm always thinking, "I got this." When, really, asking for help is exactly what I need. This reminds me [Bill] of the days before GPS. My wife and I would be driving on a road trip for vacation with our AAA Triptiks, these were step-by-step maps showing you how to get to your destination. I would regularly ignore the maps believing that I knew the way or had a short-cut that would save us a ton of time. However, you know how this one ends, we would wind up lost, and my wife kept saying, "Why don't we just stop and ask for direction," and I continued to think "I got this, and it will eventually work out." Well, hours later, I finally would stop and ask for help and discover that I was way off track and officially lost!

Leaders today are often afraid to ask for help, fearing it may be seen as a sign of weakness or that they can't do the job. Instead, I'm working to learn that asking for help is a sign of courage. Courage that is transparent enough to admit we don't know something, courage to share we are lost, or courage to overcome a weakness. By having this type of courage, we put our egos aside for the betterment of those around us. Why strug-gle and sputter along when we can get help and support instead?

Leaders are often nervous about asking for help within their organization; it's never easy asking your superintendent or supervisor for help. Can you let them know that you don't know what you are doing? By asking for help, you demonstrate you are still learning, too. However, if you don't feel comfortable asking your superiors for help, go to your professional learning network (PLN) first. This group of leaders can be an excellent think tank in solving a problem, resolving a conflict, or helping when you are lost. This reminds me of my PLN; we have a Voxer group that allows us to ask questions to other school leaders. There's about 10 school leaders in the Voxer group from all over the country. On one occasion, a principal was having an issue with a club in his school. He posed the problem on the Voxer group, and we all answered back with ideas and strategies to resolve it or simply offered support. I was encouraged by how quickly our team came together to lift up a fellow principal.

Table 8.2   Courage to Ask For Help

When I ask for help, I go to . . .	No Way	Interesting Idea	All The Time— My Go To Peeps!
Our students			
Our faculty and staff members			
My work colleagues/ peers (Other school leaders in your district)			
My professional learning network			
My supervisors			
Other			

It takes courage to risk asking others for help. Far too often, leaders go to adults they trust, but hero-building leaders are brave enough to engage students for help when appropriate. Plus, they also engage and empower their faculty/ staff by seeking guidance and support when needed. Building a professional learning network is essential to growing as a leader;

> Visit our website at www .chaselearning.org to join one of our mastermind groups and grow alongside other leaders.
>
> ©DrBillZiegler @DrDaveRamage

take time, and be intentional in connecting with leaders outside your school to grow and flourish. Join a Twitter chat, a Voxer group, or our book study to continue to learn and grow. Visit our website at http://www.chaselearning.org to join one of our mastermind groups and grow alongside other leaders.

COURAGE TO BE TRUE

Do you remember why you became a leader? I would venture a guess that you decided to become a leader to make a difference in the lives of your students, faculty, and staff. This mission needs to remain at the heart of everything we do as school leaders. We need to remain true to our convictions, hold true to our values, and model integrity in everything we do.

We need to stick to our convictions and what inspired us to be school leaders—make every decision based on what's best for students. When we hold true to these convictions, we become effective leaders who can transform a learning community and culture.

Courage to be true also focuses on the need to live a life of integrity. Having the courage to do the right things even when no one is looking is critical. This is what is generally defined as being a person of character. We need to be leaders of character, who are tirelessly committed to upholding the ideas and values we expect from our students and staff. We believe that leaders should be held to a higher standard. Our lives are constantly under a microscope, especially when we live near our school district. It's important that we model and uphold both our personal and the district values. I was recently at a large hardware box store purchasing some goods for a home renovation when I heard someone calling out my name loudly down the aisle. I could tell the calling out of my name was not one of fondness. I considered stopping in my tracks right there and turning around. But I decided that I was not going to let this obviously upset parent distract me from my shopping and in finishing my renovation. Plus, I'm not sure stopping and turning around would have worked as the parent came walking to me as soon as she saw me. I discovered it was a parent in my school who had a strong disliking for a decision that we made as a school over a discipline matter. As I walked down the aisle trying to get to the lighting department, the parent was pointing her finger at me, raising her voice, and chanting the action that she wanted me to take. I greeted the parent with a smile, and I wished her a good afternoon. This didn't stop the argumentative parent, but I was committed to showing her respect and not letting her see me get upset. Inside, I was ticked off, fired up, and wanted to engage the parent. I couldn't believe how rude and obnoxious this parent was on a Saturday, while I was standing there in my shorts with dried paint all over them, my ripped shirt, and the sneakers I use to mow the lawn, I mean I looked terrible. Now, I was starting to feel even more terrible, I was thinking, would she have done this if I had my kids with me? My better judgment won out, and I remained calm and respectful. My younger self would have given that mom a piece of my mind, but I realize now as a veteran leader that our actions directly reflect our leadership. Each day, each action, and each word represents our reputation and integrity. That's why we need to weigh our actions and words very carefully.

With courage to be true, it's important to make decisions that are best for students, not the adults in the school. We had our shot at learning, we need to focus our attention and resources on students. I'm not saying we need to ignore our faculty and staff members—that's the farthest thing from the truth. But, the decisions we make need to revolve around students, not what's going to keep adults happy. The statements below are total generalizations, we know that these statements don't hold true for all adults, but we are using them as a discussion point to get you thinking about who you make your decisions for. Adults like

- Barriers on courses so they don't have to work with a certain population of students
- The structure of school even if it sacrifices creativity and innovation
- To have the good kids in their classes
- A curriculum rather than a genius hour for students to learn about what they want
- Bells and quiet hallways rather than flexibility and talking
- Detentions and suspensions even if they aren't effective
- Paper and pencil even though their students and the world are digital
- Multiple choice tests even though they are rarely used in the real world

Table 8.3   Reflection on Courage to Be True

The decisions I make are for the benefit of . . .	Never	Sometimes	Always
Students			
Faculty and staff			
Parents			
Me			
My superiors			
Other			

- Homework even though research suggests it has little impact
- Repetition even though it may not be effective
- Giving zeroes even though it's statistically irresponsible to do so

This list could go on and on. Hopefully it serves as a primer to challenge your thinking. Be careful that you are making your decisions based on what's best for students and not adults.

COURAGEOUS CONVERSATIONS

Without a doubt, one of the hardest things to do as a leader is to have a courageous conversation with a teacher or staff member. These conversations are awkward, uncomfortable, and typically against our nature as human beings. However, these conversations are needed to move the school forward, to strengthen the school culture, and to raise the level of teaching and learning in any school. Challenging the status quo, asking tough questions, and digging into unhealthy attitudes and behaviors for the betterment of students is an important skill set for all leaders.

Figure 8.1   Seven Keys for Courageous Conversations

Do It Now
Remain Calm
Teamwork
Just the Facts
Mission Control
Let It Go
Stay Close

7
Keys

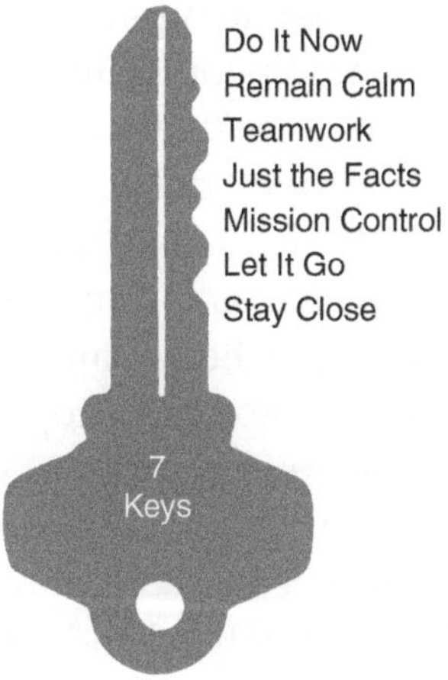

iStock.com/CSA-Archive

Work together as a team to work through the simulation in the Hero Training at the end of the chapter. This simulation will test your ability to have a courageous conversation, it will enhance your focus and skills with courageous conversations, and it will provide opportunities to collaborate around making the best decision.

The following are seven keys that we have found helpful when the need for a courageous conversation comes up.

- *Do It Now*—I can remember as a young leader putting off the difficult conversation hoping it would go away or that maybe someone else would intervene on my behalf. I found that this only made it worse and more intimidating. By waiting, I stressed over the conversation and it left too much of a gap in time. Now, after years as serving as a leader, I work to have the "courageous conversation" sooner rather than later. I find this helps me and the person I am having the conversation with. Waiting only causes anxiety. Don't be the kind of leader who schedules a meeting with the person you are planning on having the conversation with on a Monday so they have to stress and worry all weekend. This is what manipulative leaders do who work to invoke fear in people. Instead, treat the person as you would want to be treated. Hold the conversation as soon as possible, don't delay, do it today.

- *Remain Calm*—Nothing can halt the progress made in a "courageous conversation" more than the leader losing his or her temper, being sarcastic, or making snide remarks. Regardless of the topic or message, it's important to be professional, respectful, and representative of the behavior that you would like to see from your teachers. Take a minute to talk out the conversation in your head and different ways it can go. This will help you to be ready and to remain calm. Whatever you do, don't get emotional, be calm, respectful, and firm. You can send a very strong message without overreacting or becoming emotionally charged.
- *Teamwork*—Many times, these conversations are best with a colleague by your side listening and taking notes. By doing this, you document and memorialize the meeting, and you have a witness to support what you shared. Perhaps it's an assistant principal, dean of students, or even another principal from within the district that can support you with this. If you are the only leader in your building, ask a leader from another school or the district office to come over and support you. This helps in corroborating what took place, documenting the meeting, and providing another perspective. Plus, if you aren't comfortable with courageous conversations, and not many of us are, this allows you to have a support network and someone to encourage you.
- *Just the Facts*—This can be a hard one, but it's important that you stick to the facts. Too often we like to interject our own opinions, feelings, and emotions into the conversation. By sticking to the facts, the conversation focuses on the behavior that needs to change, the action

that needs to take place, or the attitude that needs adjustment. By sticking to the facts, we free ourselves from getting emotionally charged, and we focus on the mission of the meeting. I like to document the facts as I know them before the meeting and outline some general questions that I may ask during the conference. This allows me to focus on, and stick to, the facts. I have found that without these initial facts and outline of questions, it's easy to become distracted and off task. Be focused, and stick to the facts.

- *Mission Control*—Never move away from the focus of doing what is best for students. When we begin to compromise this mission of doing what's best for students, to appease adults, we slowly chisel away at the mission of serving All Students, No Matter What! This requires us to remain laser focused on the mission, vision, core values, and goals of the organization. When we steer away from these core values, we lose sight of the goal and the focus of the conversation.
- *Let It Go*—Again, as a young leader, these conversations would stick with me long after they took place. I learned that I was carrying the baggage of these conversations home with me, and it began to impact my level of joy in my role as leader. Now I focus on putting these conversations into perspective, realizing that we all need a "courageous conversation" at some point, and moving onto the next task. I work hard to not carry these conversations with me or replay them in my mind. When I continue to ponder on the conversation, I find myself either second guessing myself or looking at the person differently. It's best to have the conversation and then move on. By doing this, we free ourselves and our minds up to move forward and focus on other things. Plus, it allows us to not carry the baggage of that person with us. These conversations can weigh us down. Think of the kids that we talked about earlier carrying the invisible backpack—leaders carry a similar

backpack with the failures, defeats, struggles, and missteps that we make. We want to do everything to our best ability, and when things don't go our way, we tend to carry them with us. Carrying this around only acts as an albatross that pulls us down into the deep water. We need to throw these burdens into the deepest part of the sea and put up a "No Fishing" sign that doesn't allow us to go back and relive them. Move on, let it go, and feel the fresh air of freedom.

- *Stay Close*—Don't shy away from the person after the "courageous conversation." Treat him or her the same as you treat your best staff member. Respect them, honor them, and embrace them as a key team member. We always say leadership is about relationships, and this is where that mantra becomes a reality. Set clear expectations, expect positive results, and let them know that you believe in them and that they can change their behavior/attitude/action. By doing this, others see that failure isn't final, and it creates a culture of trust and respect. I have worked with leaders who strive to make the individuals' lives terrible; they give them the worst schedules, the most duties, or repeated recesses. Or, they ignore the person and give him or her the cold shoulder hoping the person gets the message that he or she messed up. These types of behaviors only put dividers and walls between the leader and the faculty and staff. Stop these types of childish behaviors, be mature and rise above this petty type of leadership. Instead, show care, respect, and love. That's right, I said *love* because love is willing to look past the mistakes and errors to see the best in someone.

Remember, these "courageous conversations" are not easy, but they are worth it to improve your school culture. Take a few moments and reflect on the Courageous Conversations Self-reflection, and work to identify your areas of strength and areas needing improvement.

Table 8.4   Courageous Conversation Self-Reflection Tool

	I need to grow in this area—I struggle with this.	I'm alright, but I could work to improve.	I do this sometimes.	I practice these principles regularly and consistently.
Do It Now				
Remain Calm				
Teamwork				
Just the Facts				
Mission Control				
Let It Go				
Stay Close				

COURAGE TO SHATTER THE STATUS QUO

One of my favorite hero movies is *Black Panther*. In many ways, *Black Panther* shattered Hollywood's status quo by having an African Hero, a cast with a majority of African-American actors, and an African-American director who was only 31 years old when the movie premiered. *Black Panther* went on to shatter box office expectations and quickly rose to the number one release.

When school leaders have the courage to shatter the status quo, learning, leading, and culture in schools is revitalized. If you practice the courage that we mentioned previously and join it with the courage to shatter the status quo, student learning flourishes, and your school will thrive. This type of courage requires the leader to ask the tough questions, to expose data that hurts kids, and to take action to change the thinking and practices of adults in the school.

Here's an activity for you to complete. I'd like you to review your demographic data for your school. Then, take a walk through your school visiting classes. Instead of conducting your regular walkthrough that provides feedback to the teacher, collect data on the progress of your school based on the demographics in the advanced classes you visit. Using your school's demographics, check to see if each class reflects the demographics of your school. For example, do your advanced placement, honors, and other high-level course offerings reflect the demographics of your school? Is the gender breakdown of students reflected in your high level math, science, and engineering courses? We need to work to create balance and increase opportunities for our girls just as much as we do for our boys.

Do your top level classes have the same percentage of economically disadvantaged and ethnically diverse students as your school enrollment? If your school demographics are 30 percent African-American, 20 percent Hispanic, and 50 percent white, does a high level course also have this representation? If not, leaders need to have the courage to ask why, to look for ways to change this practice, and work to overcome barriers that may be preventing students from equal access and opportunity.

Another area to examine is the disproportional discipline administered to students of diversity and economically disadvantaged students. We need to confront these issues head on and stop repeating the same mistakes over and over in how we administer discipline with these students. We need to have the courage, to examine the data, to take action, and to address the injustices to these students. The courage to stand up to this injustice and shatter the status quo is critical to helping these students find success. This requires us to directly address the biases of some adults, to shine a spotlight on the imbalance, and to act in supporting these students to find success in the school.

We talk often about shattering the status quo, but far too many schools are holding back students of diversity, economically disadvantaged students, and students with IEPs. That's right, we said we are holding back students with IEPs. How many students with IEPs are given the opportunity to take

Table 8.5   Shattering the Status Quo

	Not at All	We Need to Work on This	It's Close But Not There Yet	Yes
Do the demographics in your high level courses reflect the demographics of your school?				
Do the number and percentage of students suspended reflect your school's demographics?				
Does the number of students earning honors reflect your school's demographics?				
Do the types of students involved in extracurricular activities reflect your school's demographics?				
Does the number of students eating lunch with the principal reflect your school's demographics?				
Does the number of positive messages sent home reflect your school's demographics?				
Does the number of your grade level failure reflect your school's demographics?				
Do your numbers of truancy and unexcused absences reflect your school's demographics?				
Does the number of awards you give out reflect your school's demographics?				
Do the numbers of crossing guards and recess helpers reflect your school's demographics?				

high level courses with adjusted timelines, supports, and specially designed instruction for these students? Computer sciences courses are one example where historically struggling students can sometimes find tremendous success.

Let's work to shatter the status quo by providing opportunities for all students regardless of race, gender, religion, sexual orientation, socioeconomic status, special education designation, ability, or parental influence. Work to provide true opportunity for all students and challenge the status quo of adults.

When leaders are courageous, it provides hope for everyone around them: hope to take on obstacles bigger than them, hope to press on, hope to overcome, and hope to see a brighter future. Be a leader that brings hope, that restores someone's confidence, and that causes others to believe in the mission and goals. When leaders embrace courage, others are inspired to step up and lead, to learn, and to grow. This inspirational chain reaction can cause exponential growth with students, teamwork with faculty and staff, and parents trusting in their children's educational leaders Hope is birthed from courage. This is the type of hero strength that moves mountains and a school forward. As Michelle Obama pointed out, this kind of courage can be contagious:

> So you may not always have a comfortable life. And you will not always be able to solve all of the world's problems at once. But don't ever underestimate the importance you can have, because history has shown us that courage can be contagious, and hope can take on a life of its own. (Obama, 2011)

HERO SIGHTING

"When students can say, with evidence, 'I am a learner,' it is more likely they will invest in learning, and get pleasure from learning. It is a virtuous cycle" (Hattie & Yates, 2014, p. 219).

Reflect with your team. How are you combating years of academic struggle to help students see themselves as learners? What are the biggest obstacles to tackle for students who see themselves as nonlearners? What interventions and supports can you put in place to change the mindset for struggling students?

Taking the time to get a fuller picture of what our students bring to school that keeps them from saying "I am a learner" has a measurable impact on their success. Help turn a downward spiral into a more virtuous cycle by focusing on some of your most fragile students in a specific way. Choose a student, and use a "10/2" approach. Be sure to have two minutes of conversation or check-in with the student for ten days (class periods) in a row. This brief, consistent contact may be just enough to gain a more accurate look inside his or her backpack. Have the fortitude to frequently have this kind of courageous conversation with your students. Who knows which adult in the building may be the one who breaks through and changes the entire trajectory of a student's life? Be that hero.

HERO TRAINING

Use these activities to nurture your skills. Even better—gather with your team to embed these skills in your work and empower your students to become heroes that change their world.

1. Hero SIM—Visit our website https://www .chaselearning.org/herobuilding, and complete the 8.0 Hero Courage SIM.
2. Hero Reflections—Take time to complete reflections in Tables 8.1, 8.2, 8.3, 8.4, and 8.5. Work alone or with a team to complete these reflections, but be sure to use the findings to drive real and sustainable change in your school.
3. As a leadership team, write your school's hero story, and share it with your faculty and staff members.

Courageous Coaching—Having a courageous conversation is never easy, feel free to reach out to us, and we will support you and provide some strategies for success. Reach out to us on Twitter. @DrBill Ziegler and @DrDaveRamage

References

Boykin, C. J. (2015). *Right motives, wrong methods: Educating with poverty in mind*. ISBN: 978-0692478608

Brandt, E. (2014). A 'day in the life' of a Pottsgrove high school student. *The Reporter Online*. Retrieved from http://web.saxo .thereporteronline.com/lifestyle/20140308/a-day-in-the-life-of-a-pottsgrove-high-school-student.

Brown, P. C., Roediger, H. L., & McDaniel, M. A. (2014). *Make it stick: The science of successful learning*. Cambridge, MA: Harvard University Press.

Carey, J., & Hartleb, E. (June 2016). Virginia high school student makes 3-D printed hand for little brother. *NBC Washington*. Retrieved from https://www.nbcwashington.com/news/ local/Virginia-High-School-Student-Makes-3D-Printed-Hand-for-Little-Brother-384763421.html.

Centers for Disease Control and Prevention (CDC). (1998). Relationship of childhood abuse and household dysfunction to many of the leading causes of death in adults. *American Journal of Preventive Medicine, 14,* 245–258.

Common Sense Media. (2018). Social media, social life: Teens reveal their experiences. Retrieved from https://www.commonsensemedia.org/sites/default/files/uploads/research/2018_cs_ socialmediasociallife_fullreport-final-release_2_lowres.pdf.

Couros, G. (2016). The principal of change [Blog Post]. Retrieved from https://georgecouros.ca/blog/archives/tag/student-voice.

Dacey, J. S., & Lennon, K. H., (1998). *Understanding creativity: The interplay of biological, psychological, and social factors*. San Francisco, CA: Jossey-Bass.

Dewitt, P. M. (2017). *Collaborative leadership: Six influences that matter most*. Thousand Oaks, CA: Corwin.

Dintersmith, T. (2018). *What school could be: Insights and inspiration from teachers across America*. Princeton, NJ: Princeton University Press.

DoSomething.org, (n.d.). *11 facts about high school dropout rates*. Retrieved from https://www.dosomething.org/us/facts/11-facts-about-high-school-dropout-rates.

Dweck, C. S. (2016). *Mindset: The new psychology of success*. New York, NY: Penguin Random House.

Grant, A. (2016). *Originals: How non-conformists move the world*. New York, NY: Penguin Books.

Hargreaves, A., & Fink, D. (2006). *Sustainable leadership*. San Francisco, CA: Jossey-Bass.

Hattie, J., & Yates, G. (2014). *Visible learning and the science of how we learn*. London, UK: Routledge.

Holsen, M. (April 12, 2017). Harrisburg South trying to help clean oceans. *KELOLAND TV*. Retrieved from https://www.keloland.com/news/education/harrisburg-south-trying-to-help-clean-oceans_20180816005750361/1374124894.

Holt, J. (1995). *How children fail*. Boston, MA: Da Capo Press.

Hopeworks. (2017). *Mission statement*. Retrieved from https://hope-works.org/about.

Imagiroo. (2018). *The Kangaroo cup: A story of innovation*. Retrieved from http://www.imagiroo.com/about.

Jensen, E. (2016). *Poor students, rich teaching: Mindsets for change*. Bloomington, IN: Solution Tree Press.

Johansson, F. (2017). *The medici effect: What elephants and epidemics can teach us about innovation*. Boston, MA: Harvard Business Review.

Kohn, A. (1999). From degrading to de-grading. *High School Magazine*. Retrieved from https://www.alfiekohn.org/article/degrading-de-grading/?print=pdf.

Lassiter, C. (2017). *Everyday courage for school leaders*. Thousand Oaks, CA: Corwin.

Leslie. (2017). *The perks of procrastination*. Harvard Extension School, Professional Development. Retrieved from www.extension.harvard.edu/professional-development/blog/perks-procrastination.

National Child Traumatic Stress Network Schools Committee. (October 2008). *Child trauma toolkit for educators*. Los Angeles, CA & Durham, NC: National Center for Child Traumatic Stress

November, A. (2012). *Who owns the learning: Preparing students for success in the digital age*. Bloomington, IN: Solution Tree Press.

November, A. (2017). Write for my teacher, or publish for the world? *November Learning*. Retrieved from https://novemberlearning.com/educational-resources-for-educators/teaching-and-learning-articles/write-teacher-publish-world/.

Obama, M. (2011). *Remarks by the First Lady during keynote address at Young African Women Leaders Forum*. The White House, Office of the First Lady. Retrieved from https://obamawhitehouse.archives.gov/the-press-office/2011/06/22/remarks-first-lady-during-keynote-address-young-african-women-leaders-fo.

Quaglia, R. J., & Corso, M. J. (2014). *Student voice: The instrument of change*. Thousand Oaks, CA: Corwin.

Ramage, D. (2007). *Digital stories for professional learning: Reflection and technology integration in the classroom*. Ann Arbor: University of Michigan Press.

Resnick, M. (2017). *Lifelong kindergarten: Cultivating creativity through projects, passion, peers, and play*. Cambridge, MA: MIT Press.

Robinson, K., & Aronica, L. (2015). *Creative schools: The grassroots revolution that's transforming education*. New York, NY: Penguin Books.

Sarason, S. (1996). *Revisiting the culture of the school and the problem of change*. New York, NY: Teachers College Press.

The 41 most innovative K-12 schools in America. (October 19, 2015). Noodle. Retrieved from https://www.noodle.com/articles/innovative-schools-2015.

The IRIS Center. (2006). *RTI (part 1): An overview*. Retrieved from https://iris.peabody.vanderbilt.edu/module/rti01-overview.

Toshalis, E., & Nakkula, M. J. (2012, September). Motivation, engagement, and student voice. *Education Digest: Essential Readings Condensed for Quick Review, 78*(1), 29-35. ERIC Number: EJ999430

Venet, A. S. (2017). *Trauma-informed practices benefit all students*. San Rafael, CA: George Lucas Educational Foundation. Retrieved from https://www.edutopia.org/article/trauma-informed-practices-benefit-all-students.

Warrilow, C. (2016). What happens when lightning hits your car? *Weather Channel*. Retrieved from https://weather.com/storms/tornado/news/what-happens-when-lightning-hits-car-20140625.

Weiner, J, (2018). A forgotten hero stopped the My Lai massacre 50 years ago today. *LA Times*. Retrieved from http://www.latimes.com/opinion/op-ed/la-oe-wiener-my-lai-hugh-thompson-20180316-story.html.

Wormeli, R. (2018). *Fair isn't always equal: Assessment and grading in the differentiated classroom.* Portsmouth, NH: Sternhouse.

Ziegler, W. (2018, June 14). *How to turn a school around.* [Audio podcast]. Retrieved from https://podcasts.apple.com/us/podcast/how-to-turn-a-school-around/id1236494037?i=1000413821695.

Ziegler, W., & Ramage, D. (2012, April). Taking a risk: Sharing leadership and power. *Principal Leadership. 12*(8), 34-38.

Ziegler, W., & Ramage, D. (2017). *Future focused leaders: Relate, innovate, and invigorate for real educational change.* Thousand Oaks, CA: Corwin.

Index

Advanced mindset, 57
Adverse childhood experiences (ACES), 32
Adversity. *See* Failure; Resistance
Advocates. *See* School leaders
Agile learning, 140–141
Alien ideas, 88, 89–107
  about bells, 93–94
  about boundaries, 90–92
  about grading practices, 94–98
  about homework, 101–103
  about procrastinators, 92–93
  about repetition, 98–100
  about thinking differently, 103–106
  about tradition, 100–101
  See also Comfort zone; Innovation
Alternating daily schedules, 94
Alvarez, Nancy, 85, 86
Angelou, Maya, 17
Assignments, student choice and, 82–83
Authenticity, 14–16, 85, 113, 119
  Authentic Reflection Tool, 149 (figure)
  courage for, 147–149

empowerment for, 148
power of, 9
See also Problem-solving, real-world
Authentic skills, 141
Autonomy, student, 86
  See also Voice and choice, students'

Backpacks, invisible, 22–38
  leaders,' 157–158
Bailey, Simon, 105
Barriers. *See* Boundaries
Behavior, 31, 122–123, 153
  multi-tiered system of support (MTSS), 28
  positive behavior intervention, 29
  teaching, 29
Bells, 93–94, 153
Best practices, 105
Black, Megan, 14–16
Black Girls Code club, 6–7
Black Panther (film), 159
Block scheduling, 94
Board of School Directors, student voice and, 68, 69 (figure), 74–75
Born, Lily, 130–131

A SAGE Publishing Company

Helping educators make the greatest impact

CORWIN HAS ONE MISSION: to enhance education through intentional professional learning.

We build long-term relationships with our authors, educators, clients, and associations who partner with us to develop and continuously improve the best evidence-based practices that establish and support lifelong learning.

Leadership That Makes an Impact

LYN SHARRATT

Explore 14 essential parameters to guide system and school leaders toward building powerful collaborative learning cultures.

MICHAEL FULLAN

How do you break the cycle of surface-level change to tackle complex challenges? *Nuance* is the answer.

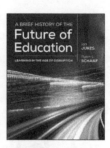

IAN JUKES & RYAN L. SCHAAF

The digital environment has radically changed how students need to learn. Get ready to be challenged to accommodate today's learners.

ERIC SHENINGER

Lead for efficacy in these disruptive times! Cultivating school culture focused on the achievement of students while anticipating change is imperative.

JOANNE MCEACHEN & MATTHEW KANE

Getting at the heart of what matters for students is key to deeper learning that connects with their lives.

LEE G. BOLMAN & TERRENCE E. DEAL

Sometimes all it takes to solve a problem is to reframe it by listening to wise advice from a trusted mentor.

PETER M. DEWITT

This go-to guide is written for coaches, leaders looking to be coached, and leaders interested in coaching burgeoning leaders.

ANTHONY KIM & ALEXIS GONZALES-BLACK

Designed to foster flexibility and continuous innovation, this resource expands cutting-edge management and organizational techniques to empower schools with the agility and responsiveness vital to their new environment.

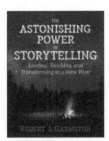